Media Translation

Media Translation

By

Mohammad Akbar

Media Translation,
by Mohammad Akbar

This book first published 2012

Cambridge Scholars Publishing

12 Back Chapman Street, Newcastle upon Tyne, NE6 2XX, UK

British Library Cataloguing in Publication Data
A catalogue record for this book is available from the British Library

ISBN (10): 1-4438-3884-5, ISBN (13): 978-1-4438-3884-9

TABLE OF CONTENTS

FOREWORD

Anyone working in the field of translation of any kind knows that it is a difficult and problematic enterprise, something that is largely unfelt by the reader or received of the translated text. It is a profession based on acquired experience, yet it can also be an art as creative as any other art. Translating from one language to another is not a matter of giving parallel words and expressions even in a scientific or documentary translation. It is, and largely in literary texts, a rendering of the spirit of the original language and the author. There are texts that no translator would aspire to translate regardless of his/her experience, talent and self-confidence. The best he could hope for is to convey meaning in a language that reflects more or less the spirit of the original text. The translator's profession is fraught with continuous anxiety and tension which are accompanied at the end with a feeling of dissatisfaction. It is also a morally and physically risky profession.

Whatever we were to say about the critical importance of translation, we would never do it justice. In this context, we have nothing to do but to remember the role played by translators over the ages by translating sciences and knowledge among nations and peoples and their role in achieving civilization and development for nations.Ancient and modern history registered famous names in the world of translation in recognition of the credit of their authors in conveying sciences and knowledge from one civilization to another and from one culture to another. This book deals with one of the aspects of translation approached by a number of Arabic books, i.e. media translation which has become more and more important in recent times. The book is divided into two chapters; in the first chapter, I have included a number of sections on the history, importance, role, progress, most important theories and types of translation; in the second chapter, I included several applications in both Arabic and English so that the professionals working in the domain of translation can make use of it, especially those working in media translation.

I wish this book, after my earlier one entitled "Television Translation" and having worked for 30 years in media translation, would be beneficial for those concerned with studying the history, art and science of translation. May it engender your career so that you acquire full command of both the languages (source language and target language). I wish also that this book would fill a vacuum in the Arabic Library in the field of translation, especially media translation.

Moreover, this book should ideally be an incentive for those working in media translation to contribute to writing books enriching the Arabic Library and provide great benefit for concerned persons and students. I would like to extend my heartfelt gratitude to all who contributed to finalizing this book and providing advice and consultation, especially Mr Samir Mas'oud who contributed with his wide-range experience over a long period and Dr Abdullah Badran who exerted great effort to follow up the work.

CHAPTER ONE

TRANSLATION HISTORY, PROGRESS AND TYPES

1.1: Translation History

There is a statement frequently quoted in almost all intellectual books: "Without translation, the world has no history". This clear and brief statement summarizes the importance of translation and sheds light on the major role played by it; studying the history of translation helps those concerned with translation, literature and cultural studies to have a better and profound understanding of the contributions made by translation in civilization and its role in the process of cultural and intellectual life development.

The reason for this is that translation is closely related to progress achieved in all fields; all the eras of awareness and renaissance in the history of nations, peoples and societies started with translation.

The French Scholar, Antoine Berman, says, "Building the history of translation is the first task of the modern translation theory."

In the modern era, civilizations became various, the scope of culture widened and sciences became ramified; it has become necessary for each nation to make full use of the heritage, culture and sciences of other nations, and to develop, enrich and utilize them for achieving the welfare of all humanity.

Thus, translation becomes a bridge linking nations that have varying degrees of development and prosperity. Hence, differences and gaps become small, and each respective heritage in every nation derives from the general human heritage.

Considering the very beginning of translation among the languages of nations and peoples, one finds that ideas and visions were imparted from one culture to another through travellers and dealers; translation gradually began to play a major role in developing the world culture.

For example, translation played a major role in imparting knowledge and sciences from Ancient Greece to Persia, from India to the Arabs, from Islam to Christianity and from Europe to China and Japan.

Then, the invention of alphabets helped authors and translators to compile and construct written languages and dictionaries; this was contributed to by the emergence of national literature and the dissemination of religions.

Translators played an effective and decisive role in achieving development and progress for their societies and in writing the history of thought itself. Over time, the task assumed by a translator gained an overriding importance in developing, activating and imparting cultural heritage to humanity.

Translation is as old as man's instinct to know, understand and be understood by others. George Monan, in a major encyclopaedia, says that there was a treaty between the Ancient Egyptians and Hittis three thousand years ago, the text of which was written in the languages of both sides and that there were translators appointed by the ruling Pharaohnic dynasties, who used to inherit this work and hold the title of a prince.

The first annals of history (some of which date back to the 11th Century BC) show considerable activity in translation, especially in China and India indicate that translation was practised by government employees whose main concern was to convey ideas.

This made the Scholar Jia Ghunghian define translation as the replacement of one written language for another without changing the meaning.

This definition, despite being a primitive one, proves the existence of a translation theory in Ancient China. However, serious discussions regarding translation were initiated only after the introduction of Buddhism in such countries in 222 – 589 AD, when the monks of Buddhism started to translate the classics of Buddhism into Chinese.

By the early fourth century, translation was organized, at a large scale in China, and a governmental school was established for translation under the administration of Daw Ann who was kidnapped to Changhan where he established his famous translation school and which became one of the most important translation centres of the time.

Three of the most prominent translators of this school adopted different techniques and theories of translation:

Daw Ann: He insisted upon strict literal translation, i.e. rendering the source text into a word-for-word translation.

Indian Scholar **Kuma Rajina**: He adopted a contrary technique, totally devoted to the free translation method which targets an elegant and comprehensible style in the language into which the text is rendered.

The Chinese Buddhist Scholar **Shwan Zhangh**, however, combined the two techniques.

The Arabs have long known the art of translation and realized its importance; they translated whatever they found proper into Arabic in the field of medicine, drugs, philosophy, literature and other sciences and arts.

In the era when translation was prosperous, it was common for the translator to receive a golden reward equalling the weight of the book he translated. Historians point out that the most professional translators (Ancient Arabs) were Aal Hunain Abu Zaid Hunain bin Isshaq (773-853), the chief translator, his son Isshaq who died in 910 or 911 AD and his nephew Jaish bin Al-A'asam. This family was widely famous and had a great reputation to the extent that many contributions were attributed to its members, with which they might have had nothing to do. In that era, the fame of Hunain was publicly known to the extent that every work of translation had the touch of Hunain by means of correction, editing or interpretation. Abbasid Caliph Al-Ma'amoun promoted him to the rank of the chief translator; he used to generously give him gifts and assign him to do critical tasks. Assistants of Hunain admitted his superiority and wide horizons of comprehension; Jibreel bin Bakhtishoo'u used to call him "Ibn Hunain", i.e. our master Hunain.

1.1.1: First Requirement: Definition of Translation

First: Linguistic Definition:

Al-tarjama is the Arabic word for translation and the Arab scholar Ibn Manzhour (died in 711 AH) said: Tarjama a derivative of Al-turjuman, is the one who interprets the utterance. In the speech of Hercules (Heracles), the term tarjama appears to mean translation.

A turjuman (translator) is the person who translates utterance, i.e. renders it from one language into another.

Among the examples not mentioned by grammarian Sibawaih: "tarjamahu (he translated it)", "tarjama hu (he translated according to it)" and "turjuman (translator)".

Second: Idiomatic Definition:

Translation is considered a main stage in the process of cognitive communication and in the relevant scientific, artistic domains. Translation has moral and ethical dimensions. It also has legal obligations and communicative objectives. There are numerous multi-dimensional objectives of communication which aim at enhancing and enriching the evaluation of a term, word, sentence or even paragraph for increasing the credibility of a translator and translation.

Translation is a science, an art and a propriety; it requires one to be accurately specialized in one of its fields so that the translator can be constantly updated and keep up with the single wording and phrase in his/her field of specialization, especially in the field which necessitates introducing an aesthetic spirit to the text as well as keeping the honesty of the correct meaning. Translation is only a main stage for the process of information communication.

So far, we have found a few contemporary authors who have provided a definition for translation, while we see old authors already referred to have approached translation as in the examples below.

The Great Man of Letters Al-Jahiz , one of the scholars of the second and third Hijri century mentioned the prerequisites for a successful translator saying: "A translator must have a great deal of knowledge in the field of translation thereof; he should have full command of both the source and target language. Whenever we find a person using two languages, we know that is unjust with one of them because each language attracts the other, takes from it and objects to it. Is the translator's mastery of two languages like the mastery of one language? A translator has one aspect of mastery; if he masters one language, it overcomes the other. If a translator uses more than two languages, the level of mastery is distributed over the number of languages. You will never find a translator **equalling** one of those scientists".

The historian and man of letters, Salah Al-Din Al-Safadi, one of the elites of the eighth Hijri century, handles translation from another perspective, saying that translation has two ways of rendering. The first way is that of Yohanna bin Al-Batreeq and Ibn Na'ema Al-Hamsi; it is to look at each single word of the Greek words and the meaning it denotes. The translator brings a single equivalent word in Arabic and selects it, and so on until he/she finishes the text he/she wants to translate. This method is bad for two reasons; the first reason is that there are lexical items in Arabic which are not equivalent to all the Greek lexical items. This is true during translation; there are many lexical items in Greek which are kept as they are without change; the second reason is that the properties of the language system and construction are not identical in two languages. Errors occur when using many figures of speech in all languages. The second approach in translation is that of Hunain bin Isshaq and Al-Jawhari, i.e. the translator grasps the meaning of the whole sentence in his mind and expresses it in an identical sentence in the other language whether lexical items are the same or different. This approach is better; therefore, the books translated by Hunain bin Isshaq did not need editing, except in the case of mathematical sciences (because he was not fully competent in them), medicine, and natural and divine logic.

Ahmad Hassan Al-Zayat, one of the contemporary leaders of translation, talked about his school of translation, saying, both, referring to what is said by Al-Jahiz and Al-Safadi, are the two schools of translation in Islam. The school I followed in all that I translated is a combination of both schools. I took advantage of combining the good aspects and confining myself to translating literary works that was not done by early translators who only handled the translation of sciences and philosophy, except for Ibn Al-Moqaffaa' and others. The feeling and emotional experience felt by the writer and poet should ideally be expressed powerfully and sincerely. I literally render the foreign text into Arabic according to its construction in its respective language. Then I contrast it with the original Arabic style, changing the order of sentences and phrases without addition or deletion and then I formulate the spirit and emotions of the author in the text through the appropriate words and figures of speech. Finally, I produce a product that the author's novel or poem in Arabic appears in a form that resembles the original text in meaning, style and emotion.

Hence, translation in this way was more difficult and exhausting because the author directly renders from his inner feelings into his own language of expression but the translator renders from a language totally different from his own language in composing the sentence, structuring the style and portraying nature and environment in the light of education, mentality and civilization. The effort of the former lies in the manipulation of the disobedient language to accept the foreign meaning in such a manner not resulting in ambiguity or dissonance. The effort of the latter lies in the blending in of what is translated from, feeling it with his heart, looking at it with his eyes and uttering it with his tongue; by this manipulation and this blending, honesty of expression and performance are achieved and thus both a translator and an author become as one person and his reflection in a mirror. (1)

Dr Mohammad Enani sees that "translation is an applied art represented in a craft polished and improved only by training and practice depending on a pre-existing talent." This means that a professor of language or literature, or both, however knowledgeable in English or Arabic, can not produce an acceptable text translated from one of the two languages without having practised translation for a long time.

Translation, as noted by Ghassan Ghosen, is a cultural interchange through conveying literary heritage from one language into another. He imposes technology, accuracy and restriction to special rules. This becomes an independent art among literary arts. It is also one of the windows of culture extending beyond the limits of environment. It exists and prospers in atmospheres where the matters and affairs of people go well. The most prominent evidence of this is that the intellectual renaissance in the Abbasi era was based on the intellectual interchange from translating Indian, Greek and Persian philosophies and sciences; thus, Arabian thinking was linked to the human thinking.

Newmark believes that "translation is a skill represented in attempting to replace a message and/or statement written in one language for a message and/or statement written into another language." Catford defines translation as, "the process of replacing the text written in one language (called Source Language) with an equivalent text written in another language (called Target Language)". By this definition, Catford focuses on the impact resulting from the written text, not just rendering the linguistic components at the level of lexical items or grammatical items.

Halliday thinks that the "textual equivalent between the source language and target language texts does not necessarily require finding the formal equivalent between both texts at the level of lexical or grammatical items; rather, it requires finding an equivalent at the entire text level."

Some researchers and scholars focus on the meaning of the term "text" in relation to translation; this is because a "text" means anything to translate whether written or oral. Text could be just a phrase, sentence, paragraph or a chapter of a book or even an entire book.

This indicates that emphasis is laid in translation on investigating the relationship between language and translation and the main aim behind this is to give translation a fixed form to follow in different cases of translation and to attempt to formulate governing rules for the purpose of preventing or avoiding mistakes when performing the process of translation.

Ghassan Ghosen gives us his opinion about Arabicization, saying, "I completely refuse to use the expression 'Arabicization' to mean translation from a foreign language into Arabic, though it is quite common as such. My references for proving what I am sticking to, on the basis of conviction not obstinacy, are numerous, of which I mention three followed by a personal note:

1- Al-Muajam Al-Wasseet Dictionary, issued by the Academy of Arabic Language in Cairo, defines the word "Arabicization" as "giving the word an Arabic form when rendering it from its foreign word into Arabic."

2- *Dictionary of Arabic Terms in Language & Literature* by Magdi Wahba and Kamel Al-Mohandes does not mention the word "Arabicization" at all; while in the chapter on translation, it mentions that it is "rewriting a certain subject into a language other than the language in which it was originally written."

3- In *Linguistic & Literary Terms Dictionary*, "Arabicization" has two different definitions: "the Arabs shall say the foreign word as it is in manner and style or the opposite". Both definitions are in agreement that the translated word is a foreign word said by the Arabs, but they differ in the conditions of this translation; the first makes it a condition that the translated word shall be changed by deletion, addition or inversion and attaching it to one of the Arabic rhythms, and the second does not provide for this condition.

This dictionary is the only one among the five references adding, without adopting, that "it is noteworthy that the word 'Arabicization' is used nowadays to mean translation from a foreign language into Arabic." (2)

Dr Subhi Al-Saleh says that Translation is not in Arabic more than rendering the meanings included by the foreign words rendered. On this consideration, translation is a common linguistic feature among Arabic and other human languages; if Arabic is not created by main languages, they all affect and get affected, lend and borrow, whenever they are linked to one another in any manner, for any reason or end.(3)

Latif Zaitouni comments on this, saying, translation is a rendering of the meaning; it handles a phrase as it handles a word making Arabic sentences and Arabic words. The Arabic sentence is the one given an Arabic formulation in the manner made by Arabs in their utterance. The Arabic words are of Arabic origin, whether ones put for directly giving the meaning or derived from an Arabic origin to give a new meaning or its old meaning was modified to imply a new. Rendering the foreign meaning into Arabic through Arabic words and Arabic sentences is the intended meaning of translation. Translation is originally of two types each of which is divided into sections, and each section is divided into branches according to the distribution of mental production and the variety of its types and arts. We give examples of this through the following figure of speech:

Translation:
1- Oral:
A- Primitive: If the language of a nation is not written.
B- Civilized: It includes, for example, the simultaneous interpretation in conferences and meetings.
2- Written:
- Divan:
- Translation of administrative memos, correspondence and press news.
- Scientific translation.
- Translation of history, philosophy, religion and sociology books.
- Literary translation.

From the above, it is clear that translation is a conveyance of an idea or informing others thereof, converting this informing into another language and giving it a written or audible form, or setting an identical form to the form in the target language. (4)

1.1.2: Second Requirement: Historical Stages of Translation

Translation went through several stages in the history of humanity. Civilizations witnessed the translation of a number of documents, registers and books from other languages into their own languages for the purpose of achieving communication with other civilizations and establishing relationships with them. Translation was the only means for each civilization to understand the language of others.

Regarding the Arabs, the stages of translation can be chronologically divided according to the following:

First: In the Pre-Islamic Era:
There is proof pointing out that the Pre-Islamic Arabs knew and practised translation; this proof includes the following:

1-   Personal Relationships:
This includes personal relationships between the Arabs and non-Arabs such as the meeting between Imroa Al-Qais and Caesar; thus, we find him reciting his poetry:

فأوجهني وركبت البريدا   ونادمت قيصر في مُلكه

I drank with Caesar in his own kingdom;
He entertained me and prepared horses for me to travel with.

We read in the books of history about the visit of Al-A'asha to Al-Hira countries and the Land of Non-Arabs and this was proved through his lines:

جزى الله إياساً خير نعمته   كما جزى المرء نوحاً بعدما شابا

في فلكه إذ تبداها ليصنعها   وظل يجمع ألواحاً وأبواباً

May Allah reward Iaas for his own favour;
In the same manner Allah rewarded Noah when he grew old.
Allah helped Noah build his Ark and collect pieces of wood;

Likely, the relationship between the elite of the Arabs with Al-Monthir bin Al-No'aman was portrayed.

This clearly proves that there is an oral interpretation made by the Pre-Islamic Arabs. (5)

2- Business Relationships:

As it is known, some tribes such as the Quraish had business relationships with India, China, Persia, Rome, Ethiopia, Al-Hira Government, Ghassanides; this made Mecca a terminal on the route of caravans.

3- International Relationships:

An example of international relationships is that Udai bin Zaid worked as an ambassador for Hormoz bin Anoshrowan to Caesar Tiberius and was succeeded in his post by his son Zaid. Two of his brothers also worked in the same profession. Zaid, father of Udai, used to read both Arabic and Persian. Luqait bin Ya'amor Al-Yaadi wrote to Caesar of Persia and translated for him. The conquests of Alexander the Great were historical ones with which cultural interchange was made. In this regard, Dr Jawad Ali says, "Alexander's conquests, which threw the Greeks and Romans to vast areas of Asia, are not only a political event; rather, they are one of the chapters of human history in which we read the news of both the Eastern and Western Worlds encountering each other face to face on vast areas of land; the tendency of the West to assume hegemony over the East; the civilizations being influenced by one another; Greek and Roman scientists gaining direct knowledge about the conditions of nations they used to hear about from dealers, tourists and navigators. If you reach such nations, there is an end to the element of imagination tending to exaggeration and overestimation. The conquests of Alexander corrected some such misconceptions for the Fertile Crescent and Egypt. Such conquests brought the scholars and scientists of Greece to these countries, especially Egypt. They received and gave benefits and Alexandria, in particular, and some of the Levant Countries, became the meeting place of cultures, both Eastern and Western and the intellectual contact centre between the West and East; Alexandria continued to keep its rank till the adoption of Islam." (6)

4- Religion:

Religion played a major role in reviving the movement of translation; hence, Mecca, as a religious centre, became a main stopping point on the caravan route. Churches played a vital role in the process of cultural interchange. Missionaries also played an effective role in the process of translation; they rendered the Greek and Aramaic heritage to the Arab Peninsula in the days of the Pre-Islamic Era.

It was proved that the Torah was translated into Arabic in the Pre-Islamic Era. This caused poets to use words which were not known in their environment. For example, Udai bin Yazeed composed some Torah stories in his poetry in Arabic:

إلى ساعة في اليوم أو في ضحى الغد   أعاذل ما يدريك أن منيتي

أمامي من مالي إذا خف عودي   ذريني فإنما لي ما مضى

تروح له بالواعظات وتغتدي (7)   كفى زاجراً للمرء أيام دهره

Perhaps I may attain my death at a certain time in the day or tomorrow morning;
Leave me to myself to feel sad for what I lost in the past;
It is enough for man to have the days as a deterrent for him.

This was also done by Umaiya bin Al-Sallt who derived the idea of the serpent story from the scriptures of the Torah and expressed it in his poetry, saying:

وذي الجني أرسله يساب   كذي الأفعى يربيها لديه

ولا الجني أصبح يستتاب (8)   فلا رب البرية يأمننها

Like the owner of serpent he breeds it with him;
And like the magician of a Jinn sent him for his own service;
Neither the Lord of World renders it secure nor the Jinn will repent;

Likely, Al-Scmoucl, making use of the ideas of previous religions, said:

إذا المرء لم يدنس من اللؤم عرضه   فكل رداء يرتديه جميل (9)

If a man is not marred by meanness, he would be good in any way he looks.

5- Scholars:

Pre-Islamic people used to travel to other countries to learn philosophy, medicine and other sciences. One of them was Zaid who sent his son Udai to learn the Persian Language in Persia, where he later became an ambassador. Also, Al-Harith bin Kalda sent his son Al-Nazhir to Jend Yasabour School in Persia. (10)

It is natural that the language of study in such countries was not the Arabic Language; it was Persian, Syriac or Greek. The dialogue between the teachers and students would be through translation.

6- Existence of Some Foreign Words:

Some foreign words were used by the Pre-Islamic people; for example, Imraa Al-Qais said:

أتت حجج علي بعدها فأصبحت   كخط (زبور) في مصاحف رهبان

Years elapsed one after the other and I became like a line of Salter in the Books of Monks.

The word "Zabur" (Salter) is not an Arabic word; it is Hebrew.
Another example of Imraa Al-Qais is when he says also:

مهفهفة بيضاء غير مفاضة   ترائبها مصقولة كالسجنجل (11)

The word used in the above text "Sajanjal" (mirror) is not an Arabic word; it is a Roman word meaning mirror.

Also, we have Al-Nabegha Al-Thobiani saying:

محلتهم ذات الإله ودينهم   قديم فيما يرجعون غير العواقب

The word "mahalla" is not an Arabic word; rather, it is a Hebrew word meaning place or position.

Dr Jawad Ali lists a group of such foreign words which Arabs used in their poems, letters and prose, thus indicating to what extent the Arabs influenced and were influenced by others. For example:

The following words:

آس	Basis
حندقوق	A type of plant (called Barbeer in Arabic)
ريحان	Basil
شالم	A type of plant
يتوع	A type of plant containing liquid
الحريز	Cautious
الاسفنط	Grape wine
نرجس	1 - A kind of plant 2 - Narcissus
تابوت	Coffin, casket
جرّ	Dragging
بطيش	Oppressor
الطباهج	Sliced meat
الجلاب	Flower water
بركان	1 - Fur 2 - Black garment 3 - Volcano
طليسان	1 - An area in Iran called Talesh nowadays 2 - Black shiny garment
موبذ	Chief justice
درهم	Dirham
فلوس	Fish skin – scales
قنطار	Pound

Second: Translation in the Early Islamic Era:

In the Era of Prophet Mohammad (PBUH), and Rightly-Guided Caliphs afterwards, the volume of communication with other nations increased because Prophet Mohammad (PBUH) did not come for the Arabs in particular, but for all the people in the universe as was the Qur'an and Islamic Sharia, as mentioned in the Holy Qur'an:

"وما أرسلناك إلا رحمة للعالمين" (الأنبياء: 107)

"Indeed we sent you only as mercy for all the people in the universe."

It was mentioned in the Prophet's Biography (Sira) that Prophet Mohammad (PBUH) sent messengers with letters to the kings and Caesars; he sent Amro bin Umaiya Al-Dhamari to Al-Najashi, King of Ethiopia; sent Haiya bin Khalifa to Caesar of Rome; sent Abdullah bin Huthafa to the Prince of Persia; sent Hateb bin Balt'aa to Al-Moqowqas the leader of Egypt; sent Shojaa bin Wahb to Al-Hareth Al-Ghassani and sent Sulait bin Amro to Saheb Al-Yamama.

For example, Al-Hafiz bin Qaiyem Al-Jawziya narrated, Prophet Mohammad (PBUH) wrote letters to Al-Moqawqas, King of Egypt and Alexandria saying 'In the Name of Allah Most Merciful, Most Compassionate: From Mohammad, bondman of Allah and His Messenger to the Great Al-Moqawqas, ruler of Copts, peace of Allah be upon him who follows the right path. I do hereby invite you to convert to Islam; convert to Islam and you will be safe; convert to Islam and you will obtain your retribution twice from Allah. If you shun, you will have the sin of Copts upon you: (Say (O Muhammad PBUH): "O people of the Scripture (Jews and Christians): Come to a word that is just between us and you, that we worship none but Allah, and that we associate no partners with Him, and that none of us shall take others as lords besides Allah. Then, if they turn away, say: "Bear witness that we are Muslims".

(قُلْ يَا أَهْلَ الْكِتَابِ تَعَالَوْا إِلَى كَلِمَةٍ سَوَاءٍ بَيْنَنَا وَبَيْنَكُمْ أَلاَّ نَعْبُدَ إِلاَّ اللَّهَ وَلا نُشْرِكَ بِهِ شَيْئًا وَلا يَتَّخِذَ بَعْضُنَا بَعْضًا أَرْبَابًا مِنْ دُونِ اللَّهِ فَإِنْ تَوَلَّوْا فَقُولُوا اشْهَدُوا بِأَنَّا مُسْلِمُونَ" (آل عمران : 64)

Prophet Mohammad sent this letter with Hateb bin Abi Balt'aa; when the latter was allowed in to Al-Moqowqas, he said to him, "There was a man before alleging that he is the supreme lord of the universe and Allah the Almighty took revenge upon him; so, it is better for you to take example from others not to let others take example from you."

Al-Moqowqs said, "We have a religion that we would never abandon except to one which is better than it."

Hateb said, "We do hereby call you to convert to the religion of Allah, i.e. Islam which has nothing parallel to it now. This Prophet called people to convert to Islam but he encountered the most cruel people of Quraish and most hostile people of the Jews, but the closest ones were the Christians. I swear the prophecy and glad tidings made by Moses for Jesus is like that of Jesus for Mohammad. Our call to you for Qur'an is like your call to the people of the Torah to the Bible. If a prophet reaches a group of people, they become his nation and they should obey him and you were reached by this Prophet. We are not preventing you from the religion of Jesus but we are commanding you with it."

Al-Moqowqas said, "I considered the matter of this Prophet and I found that he never ordained for something desirable nor prohibited doing something desirable. I do not find him a magician, nor a hypocrite or liar. I found signs of prophethood by revealing what is hidden [12] and informing of confidential talk and I will consider his matter."

Then, Al-Moqawqas took the letter of Prophet Mohammad (PBUH) and put it in an ivory box and sealed it. (13)

Prophet Mohammad (PBUH) played a major role in the movement of translation, as narrated by Zaid bin Thabet, saying, Prophet Mohammad (PBUH) said, 'I am writing to a people and I fear that they might add to or delete the contents of my letters; so, learn the Syriac language.' He said, "I learned it within seventeen days."

Moreover, letters came to Prophet Mohammad (PBUH) in Syriac; he ordered Zaid to translate them into Arabic and then Zain used to write replies to them. Zaid wrote letters for Abi Bakr and Omar. Like Zaid, Mo'aiqeb Al-Diousi used to do the same. [14]

Thus, history proves that translation used to play a major role in the intellectual life of people. The first Hijri century was a first of reception stages. For example, Omar bin Al-Khattab kept a piece of the Torah; when Prophet Mohammad (PBUH) saw him, he forbade him to keep it.

There was a strong friendly relationship established between the Arabian Muslim Ruler Umair bin Said and Patriarch John II who, in reliance on the Ruler's request, translated the Bible Scriptures into Arabic. The Patriarch delegated for this mission translators from Bani Uqail, Tanookh and Taiee. The first Arabic translation for the New Testament was done in the monastries of Al-Riqqa and Peninsula in 413 Hijri. (15)

Thus, Muslims made great use of People of the Book; they were influenced by other cultures through translation. As narrated by Abu Hurairah, People of the Book used to read the Torah in Hebrew and interpret it into Arabic for the people of the Levant.

Thus, Mecca and Medina were two centres for the Jews, Ethiopians, Persians and Byzantines. He used to speak their own languages; Friends of Prophet Mohammad (PBUH) learned their languages. Zaid bin Thab (May Allah be pleased with him) knew Persian, Roman, Coptic and Hebrew languages and used to translate for Prophet Mohammad (PBUH) the wording of all those languages; Abdullah bin Amro bin Al-A'as also mastered the Syriac Language.

When Hormozan, one of the non-Arab rulers, came to Omar bin Al-Khattab, Moghira worked as an interpreter for Omar and him and answered all the questions in Persian.

It was mentioned in the book entitled *Al-Farooq* (Omar bin Al-Khattab was called Al-Farooq as he discriminated between what is right and what is not right) that Omar bin Al-Khattab used to have meetings with Persian people to tell them about the policies of Kings, especially non-Arab kings such as Anoshrwan. They used to like it very much.

For example, it was narrated by Ibn Al-Qafeti, A Greek philosopher was allowed into Amro ibn Al-A'as, after Egypt was conquered, and they discussed philosophical issues. The philosopher was allowed in to Amro bin Al-A'as and it was known how much knowledge and belief he had and what happened to him with the Christians. Amro was generous with him and listened to him talking about the nullification of Pagan Talaiyoth doctrine and he liked it. He also listened to the philosopher talking about the elapse of time and admired his logical reasoning very much. He listened to his philosophical words which had never been known by the Arabs. Amro was wise, a good listener and was smart; he kept the philosopher beside him all the time.

There are lots of narratives showing how much Muslims influenced and were influenced by other people through translation. (16)

Third: Translation in the Umayyad Era:
With the preoccupation of Umawis with the spreading of Islam made conquests and supporting the aspects of the Islamic State, translation would have had vaster horizons. It had some important steps; it started in the Umayyad Era when the first Caliph, Mu'awia bin Abi Sofian (died in 60 Hijri), acceded to the throne. It was known that Mu'awia was fond of reading about the biographies of kings and their policies. He appointed for himself a translator (Ibn Athaal) to translate for him the books of medicine from Greek into Arabic. Mu'awia also appointed men to copy the books translated from Greek, Latin and Chinese, especially after receiving a present from the King of China. The present was a book which was translated during his reign. Then, the Umayyad Prince Khaled bin Yazeed bin Mu'awia (died in 85 Hijri) came and failed to become the Caliph. He turned away to science and gathered about it all that is related to translation. As narrated about him by Ibn Al-Nadeem, Khaled was called the Wise Man of Aal Marawan. He was a virtuous person, enthusiastic and fond of knowledge and science. He had an idea struck in his mind about craft (san'aa); he ordered that a group of Greek philosophers be brought, from among those who used to travel to Egypt and have mastery of the Arabic language. He ordered them to render the books on craft from Greek and Coptic into Arabic; this was the first thing to be translated in Islam from one language into another. (17)

Mohammad Kurd Ali mentions that Khaled used one of the scholars of the Alexandria School (Istafen) in rendering some Greek medical books into Arabic. [18]

The Greek orientialist Nillino sees that perhaps the first book rendered from Greek into Arabic was *Ahkaam Al-Nujoom* (Provisions of Stars), affiliated to Wiseman Hormos.

It is without doubt that Khaled made great use of the great library he inherited from his grandfather Mu'awia in addition to gaining knowledge and science from his master, the Damascene Marr John, who was a friend and childhood companion of his father Yazeed.

Marr John and another monk translated for him from the Greek language. Moreover, some books were translated for him from Persian by Jabala bin Salem.

One of the merits of Khaled bin Yazeed was that he made lots of the books which were translated, in the fields of astronomy, medicine, philosophy and craft, available in public libraries to be accessed by students and concerned persons.

In addition, Khaled had lots of knowledge in literature; he was an orator, fluent, having sound judgement and had soul-stirring poems.

Thus, it can be said that the library of Umayyad Caliph Mu'awia was considered the first centre for translation into Arabic. Khaled bin Yazeed developed such a central library which was called the House of Wisdom. He enriched it with books of Hadith (Prophetic Tradition), chemistry, astronomy, medicine and philosophy. He established a movement for translation therein for translating foreign books into Arabic. He gathered scholars and scientists in different fields; he thus gave the House of Wisdom its special nature.

In the reign of Marawan bin Al-Hakam (died in 65 Hijri), he appointed a Jewish physician for himself called Masserjewaih who rendered the first medical book into Arabic. The book was entitled *Kanash*, written by the Monk Ahran; it contained thirty articles. Monk Ahran was one of the physicians who lived in Alexandria during the reign of Heraql (641 AD).

Ibn Abi Usaibi'aah says, Caliph Omar bin Abdul-Aziz, may Allah have mercy upon him, ordered that the book *Kanash* be published after it was found in the storerooms of books in the Levant.

However, the problem here lies in the fact that Marawan bin Al-Hakam was preoccupied with suppressing sedition; he did not pay attention to the fact that some divans in the Umayyad State had Syriac and Persian as the prevailing languages. His son Abdul-Malek tried to draw his attention to this fact but could not do this until he became a caliph. He appointed

Sulaiman bin Saad Al-Khashni to be in charge of Levant Divan and assigned him to render it into Arabic.

During the Umayyad Era, divans were rendered from Greek into Arabic in Syria during the reign of Caliph Abdul-Malek bin Marawan; from Persian into Arabic in Iraq and beyond it by Al-Hajjaj bin Youssef, the ruler appointed by Caliph Abdul-Malek; and from Coptic into Arabic in Egypt by Abdul-Aziz bin Abdul-Malek, then ruler of Egypt. (19)

There is no doubt that rendering divans was very influential in supporting the foundations of the Arab State; Arabic became the language of management all over the territory and there was no longer the current prevailing saying that Arabic was not good for that.

The trend of translation continued in the reign of Hisham bin Abdul-Malek (died in 105 Hijri), when more than one book was translated for him. He had people to translate or proofread such as Abu Al-Alaa Salem bin Abdul-Malek who translated the messages of Aristotle to Alexander from Greek into Arabic. (20)

Likely, Jabala bin Salem translated the book of *Rostom Wasfendiar* from Persian and the book of *Bahram Shoos*, and both books were on history and politics.

Abdullah bin Al-Moqaffaa' was one of the translators who appeared at the end of the Umayyad Caliphate; he was the contemporary of about ten caliphs of Abbasid. He translated lots of Persian books into Arabic such as *Kalila and Demna, Khuway Namah, Aaeen Namah and Book of the Crown in the Biography of Anoshruwan*. He also translated the three books of logic written by Aristotle before he was killed in 142 Hijri.

One of the translators who appeared in the Umayyad Era was Hassan bin Abi Senan Al-Anbari, who used to write in Arabic, Persian and Syriac. To Hassan was attributed the translation of the book entitled *Ardh Moftah Al-Nujoom* (Review of Stars Key) which was said to have been written by Wiseman Hormos; the book revolves around the world of stars.

At the very end of the Umayyad era, the trend of translation was not that prosperous and the countdown started for the decline of the Umayyad Caliphate; however, this did not mean that translation and authoring came to an end.

Fourth: Translation in Abbassi Era:

People knew of the translation of religious books into Arabic in the Pre-Islamic Era and this was also the case for the very early years of the Islamic Era; however, the trend began to widen its scope in the Era of Rightly Guided Caliphs. Whereas in the Umayyad Era, there were some individual attempts at translating some practical sciences such as medicine and astronomy, regarding the Abbasid Era, with the spread of prosperity and stability, the Caliphate had its scope widened in space and time, thus leading to supporting the Abbasids State. Therefore, the trend of translation from and into Arabic became prosperous. This era can be divided into three stages:

1-   First Stage (136 – 193 Hijri):
    This stage is the beginning of the origination stage. It was characterized by the translation of scientific books including mathematics, medicine and astronomy. This was due to the fact that the Caliph Abu Jaafar Al-Mansour was suffering from a disease in his stomach. Therefore, he began to investigate any books coming to him from physicians; he was very concerned with translation and recruited Georgeoos bin Bakhteshiou' from Jandisapur School and assigned Ibn Batriq to translate many books, especially books from India such as the book entitled *Shanaq* in toxicology, etc.

    Abu Jaafer is considered to be the first caliph to make correspondence with the King of Rome, requesting books of wisdom from him, and the King of Rome in turn sent him the book of Iqlidis and some books on natural sciences.

    He gathered around himself the cream of scientists in different branches of knowledge, encouraged the translation of sciences and created a divan for translation.

    In the reign of Al-Mansour, the Abbasids State was concerned with translating books of astronomy and astrology. The Caliph requested the Empire of Byzantium to send him the Greek manuscripts and books they had. They sent them to him; in 771 AD, a delegation came from Sindh in the west of India, and among the persons in the delegation was a man called Kanaka who was very skilled in mathematics and astronomy. He was carrying with him a book entitled *Soria Sadhanta*. Caliph Al-Mansour ordered that such a book be summarized and then translated into Arabic; he assigned this work to Ibrahim bin Habib Al-Ghazawi, the astrologer who mastered the Hindi language, and this book was known as *Sindh Hind*.

    In addition, religious books were translated for the Manichaeism and Magianism which spread skepticism and atheism!

    It was said that Caliph Al-Mansour was the one who established the House of Wisdom in Baghdad. He was the one who endangered the public treasury when he used to pay translators in gold equal to the weight of a book translated.

Thus, translation began to prosper in the reign of Al-Mansour after the aspects of the Abbasids Caliphate were well supported. When Al-Mahdi became the Caliph, his concern was focused upon replying to disbelief, atheism and scholastic theology; he also followed in the footsteps of his father in enhancing his relationship with the physicians of Jandisapoor who translated books of mathematics and medicine for him.

When Haroon Al-Rasheed became the Caliph, translation prospered more than ever because Haroon was very fond of Greek sciences. He sent his agents to different parts of the Roman Empire to buy Greek manuscripts, especially medical ones. He spent lots of money in achieving this purpose. During his reign, Aristotle's books on logic were translated. The book of Iqlidis was translated in his reign by Al-Hajjaj bin Youssef bin Matar; the translations made in the reign of Haroon Al-Rasheed were called Harooni to be distinct from Ma'mouni Translation. In addition, the book entitled *Al-Majasti*, written by Ptolemy, was translated into Arabic under the auspices of Yahia bin Khaled Al-Barmaki.

One of the characteristics of the reign of Haroon Al-Rasheed was that the interest in translation was not limited to the caliph, prince or governor; rather, the rich turned to this trend and established centres concerned with rendering books into Arabic after bringing them from Roman countries and calling upon people to translate them.

One of the most prominent families was that of Moosa bin Shaker: Mohammad, Ahmad and Al-Hassan, who devoted a house to translation in Baghdad. It is mentioned that the most famous people who worked therein included Hunain bin Isshaq, Jaish Al-A'asam and Thabet bin Qurrah. Each of them used to receive five hundred dinars for rendering and editing.

The family of Barmaki made great contributions in the field of translation. They endeavoured to spread Persian culture in the Islamic Countries. Therefore, they ordered the precious sciences to be rendered into Arabic. They appointed, for this purpose, translators such as Al-Fadhel bin Nobakht.

Among the most prominent men in the Barmaki Family was Yahia bin Khaled Al-Barmaki, who supported such contributions from Persian; Mohammad bin Abdul-Malek Al-Zayat, who used to pay at least two thousand dinars monthly for copiers and translators; and Ibrahim Al-Kateb, who was keen on rendering the books of the Greeks into Arabic. (21)

Haroon Al-Rasheed assigned Yohanna bin Masawaih, who was the chief translator then, to translate the books he found in Ankara and Amoria during his conquests. As mentioned by Ibn Al-Nadeem, Yohanna bin Masawaih was Christian in religion and Syriac; he was assigned by Al-

Rasheed to translate old books found in Ankara and Amoria and all the Roman countries, when Muslims took them over, and was assigned by Al-Rasheed to be in charge of translation. (22)

Al-Rasheed also entrusted the affairs of the House of Wisdom's storeroom of books to Al-Fadhel bin Nobakhet Abu Sahel, of Persian origin, who mastered Persian and used to render the books he found in House of Wisdom from Persian into Arabic.

Then came the reign of Caliph Al-Amin; he was known for nothing in this field but his interest in medicine in extension of his father's concern for it. Therefore, his reign is regarded as a period of relative stagnancy. Anyhow, Al-Amin did not have sufficient time to show his contribution in prominently serving the Islamic Caliphate. It seemed that the time when he came was going in the opposite way to the one Al-Amin wanted to go through. However, there were some scientific contributions in the trend of translation. Among the most prominent persons who worked for Al-Amin in the field of translation was Jabreel bin Bakhteshiou', the grandson of Georegeoos bin Bokhteshiou'.

2-   Second Stage (198 – 300 Hijri)

Caliph Al-Amin, who remained in power for twenty years, was known to be fond of researching and debating. Therefore, he used to gather scientists and men of intellect to hold debates in front of him and to share them. Historian Sa'ed Al-Andalosi described him, saying, When the caliphate was transferred to the seventh caliph, i.e. Abdullah Al-Ma'moun bin Al-Rasheed, he completed what was initiated by his grandfather, Al-Mansour. He endeavored to find knowledge from its genuine sources thanks to his honorable enthusiasm and virtuous person. He paid visits to the kings of the Roman Empire and extended luxurious and lavish gifts to them. He asked them about their relation to the books of philosophers they kept; they sent him most of the books they had, including books of Plato, Aristotle, Hippocrates, Galileo, Iqlidis and Ptolemy, etc. He procured the most skillful translators and assigned them to translate such books. The books were translated as accurately as possible; he urged people to read them and learn them. Thus, science was prosperous in his reign and the State of Wisdom flourished; men of wits competed in sciences due to the generous gifts he used to give to those who were competent. He used to have meetings with them and get entertained by their information and they became used to high ranks and generous giving. The same happened with most scientists, jurists, philosophers, linguists and poets; some men of arts mastered many parts of philosophy and laid thereafter the methodologies of medicine and the foundations of literature to the extent that the Abbasid

State was successfully competing with the Roman Empire during its prosperity and welfare. (23)

Caliph Al-Amin was concerned with missions to the Roman Empire for obtaining books. In this regard, Ibn Al-Nadeem says, There were communications between both Al-Ma'moun and the King of Rome. Al-Ma'moun asked him to exhaust the old books of sciences, stored in his country, he selected and the Roman king reluctantly accepted. Al-Ma'moun sent a group for this purpose including Al-Hajjaj bin Matar and Ibn Al-Batriq, and they took all the books they deemed fit and proper.

Al-Ma'moun even went beyond this; he made the condition of reconciliation with the Romans to obtain the old and precious books. One of the conditions of reconciliation between Al-Ma'moun and the Byzantine Emperor Mikhael III was that the latter was to assign one of the famous libraries in Al-Qostantinia; one of its repertoires was the book of Ptolemy in astronomy, and Al-Ma'moun ordered that this book be translated into Arabic.

Al-Ma'moun established the House of Wisdom in Baghdad; it is a scientific academy, an astronomical observatory and public library where a group of translators stayed and were given their salaries from the treasury. (23)

Historians say about the House of Wisdom, It is like a scientific academy; it was divided into several departments: for copying, authoring, astronomical research and as an observatory. The whole House of Wisdom, with all its divisions, was put under the supervision of one or two scientists. Sahel bin Haroon was one of those with supervision over this institution; he was the librarian of Al-Ma'moun's own library then.

Each section had its own chief; the House of Wisdom was arranged according to the well-known Bibliotheca Alexandrina in terms of objectives, means and work methodology. It continued its work after Al-Ma'moun, though it lost much of its activity until the time of Ibn Al-Nadeem, Author of Index, in the mid-fourth Hijri century. It is likely that the House of Wisdom continued throughout the Abbasid era; it was destroyed by Holako in 656 Hijri when he occupied Baghdad.

Thus, Al-Ma'moun could make translation an organized official work of the State activities. Ibn Abi Usaibi'aa mentioned that Al-Ma'moun admired Hunain bin Issaq so much that he gave him gold weighing as much as the weight of the books he translated into Arabic. He said, I found many books among these books and I kept many of them for myself; they were written in Kufi by Al-Azraq, copier of Hunain. They were big letters written in thick handwriting on separate lines; each paper of them was as thick as three or four papers. Hunain intended, through doing this, to glorify the size of a book, making its weight heavy in order to have as many dirhams as its weight. Because such pages of paper were very thick, they could last for many years. (25)

One can not forget what was done by the rulers of Al-Andalus regarding translation; they encouraged it, were concerned for books, kept them and translated them into Arabic. In his statement about Ibn Jiljil, Ibn Abi Usaibi'aa mentioned that when Armianos, King of Constantinia, wanted to send a gift to Caliph Al-Nasser bin Abdul-Rahman bin Mohammad in Cordova, he made the book of Dasqoridis in his gift; this book contained a description for herbal medicines in Greek.

Al-Nasser appreciated this gift well; and since he did not have any one in his country to translate this book from Ancient Greek into Arabic, he asked Armianos, Emperor of Byzantine, to send him a person to translate it. The Emperor sent him Monk Niqola, who arrived in Cordova in 340 and assisted in translating the book into Arabic, especially the names of drugs. (26)

There was successive concern shown by other caliphs; for example, in the reign of Al-Watheq Billah, there were a large number of translators available from among the philosophers, as he always loved creativity. In this regard, Al-Mas'oudi said, Al-Watheq always loved contemplation; he did not like imitation. He used to supervise the sciences of people and their opinions including philosophers and physicians who made progress and others who lagged behind; thus, types of their sciences were conducted in his presence in natural sciences and divine sciences. (27)

In the reign of Al-Mutawakkel, several books were translated under the auspices of Hunain. In the reign of Al-Mosta'een Billah, Qesta bin Looqa Al-Baa'labaki was summoned to translate Greek books. Whereas for Al-Moqtader Billah, he sent a delegation of Arab physicians to India so that they could bring beneficial drugs for the diseases.

3-   Third Stage (300 – 656 Hijri):

This stage is a stage of revision for that openness for sciences which reached its climax in the reign of Al-Ma'moun, thus having its reflections upon doctrine and religion; a complete revision was made for translators, their inclinations and popularity.

Therefore, a large number of scientists, who were concerned with revising the imparted knowledge for the sake of deepening the idea of originality; it was indeed a time of creativity where the process of authoring overcame copying. This is in addition to the great transformation in translation; there was little concern with translating philosophical books and there was a great concern for translating literary books, especially the literature of Persia. Matta bin Younis, Senan bin Thabet and Ibn Zar'aa were among the most prominent translators.

This was accompanied by imparting the sciences of Muslims to other neighbouring nations such as India, China and Europe. Therefore, scientific centres increased, especially libraries, such as the library established by Abu Al-Qassem Jaafar bin Hamdan Al-Mooseli in Al-Mosul in 373 Hijri and made it exclusively for the students.

This also includes, for example, the house established by Ibn Habban in Nesapoor City, which was made a storeroom for books and housing for strangers.

Another example was the library of Al-Sharif Al-Radhi, which he took as a centre for science and opened it for students.

In addition, there were the schools of Fiqh (jurisprudence) which were established as live evidence for creativity and originality, instead of merely translating. Such schools achieved great progress, especially during the reign of Al-Mostazhir; this includes, for example, the contributions made by Abu Hamed Al-Ghazali especially in his books entitled *Tahafot Al-Falasefa* (Incoherence of Philosophers) and *Ihiaa Uloom Al-Din* (Renovation of Sciences of Religion).

A similar example was the contributions made by Al-Shahrestani, especially in his encyclopaedia entitled *Al-Melal wa Al-Nehal* (Nations and Sects).

However, this does not mean that the trend of rendering was stopped or declined, but it means that there was regulation and editing of what was being transferred in order to be compatible with the Qur'an and Sunna.

Thus, historical facts assert that no sooner had the Abbassi Era come to its end, than all the philosophical, medical, astronomical, mathematical and scientific books had become known in Arabic. People could then do without translation and were preoccupied with creativity, authoring and innovation and could reach its apex. (28)

Fifth: Translation in Renaissance Era:

The constant presence of translation, spatially and chronologically, had several reasons, including:

- **Need**: The need could be religious, scientific or political, etc. For example, the trend of translation in the Abbasids Era ensued as a result of need because Muslims were not competent in medicine and philosophy; therefore, they recruited translators and relied on other books.

- **Taste**: This includes for example, the large amount of love and detective stories which were rendered into Arabic by translators, for the sake of enjoyment and satisfying tastes.
- **Culture**: Culture is one of the reasons as it grows with the increase of a nation's openness to other nations. Therefore, translation was made from other languages into Arabic so that the Arabs could get to know the culture of Indians and others.

In addition, the Holy Qur'an and Prophetic Hadith urged us to learn, think and research. This requires translation of lots of sciences; then ensue the issue of Arabs' contact with other nations, the Arabs' need for sciences and the sponsorship of caliphs, especially the Abbassides, for translation and translators, taking into consideration the religious controversies and debates, and all this encouraged translation.

Thus, the issue developed until the 19th Century when Europe was still living in unparalleled darkness and ignorance. If we go back to the contact between Arabs and Muslims in Al-Andalus, we will notice how Europeans had Al-Andalus as their destination as if it were the Kaaba of science to which students and concerned lovers of science knowledge perform hajj.

As a result of translating into Latin, the Europeans rendered the most important Arabic books in such arts. Tolaitela City (Toledo) was the most important centre which was the destination of Europeans for this purpose.

Historically, it is known that the trend of translation continued to progress during the thirteenth century AD; during this century, universities were established in Europe. This contributed to more interest in the Arabic language, especially after classes were established for the Arabic language particularly in the universities of Paris, Oxford, Bologna and Salamancar; this trend oscillated between activity and inactivity until the middle of the eighteenth century.

All this concerned translation from Arabic into Latin, whereas translation from Latin into Arabic was carried out in several institutes including, for example, the Roman Maroon Institute. For preparation for this institute, Father John Eliano, dispatched by Pope Gregorioos XIII, came to Lebanon and published several books which were translated into Arabic, the first of which was the book entitled *Christian Tradition* by the Jesuit Peter Ketezious, and it was printed in Karshooni letters in April, 1580, then the book by Pope Luis Al-Ghernati in the Secrets of Repentance and Oblation, Laws of Tradintine Society and Constitution of Orthodox Secretariat, whose translation was reprinted after it was initially printed in 1566.

Perhaps this was the first translation from a European language; rather, there is no doubt that it is so, because nobody in Lebanon, seemingly, knew European languages in this era. The evidence for this is that Patriarch Michelle Razzi did not find anybody mastering Latin in Lebanon, though it was the language of writing and the church all over Europe then, to translate for him a message from Pope Gregorioos XIII and messages from Cardinal Crava received by him in March, 1577. Therefore, he had to wait until Pope Eliano arrived in 1578 to assign him to translate them.

Thus, the first translations into Arabic were religious, and it remained the same remained until the nineteenth century.

The book, whether translated or compiled, is to be read; therefore, it should meet the needs of the readership. The concern of all during that time was religious because of the general atmosphere created by the flow of missionaries to the East. Therefore, it is rare to find a book translated for a purpose other than religion, and most of these books were translated from Latin, Greek and some from Italian.

These books include *Christian Tradition* by Cardinal Bellarmin, translated by Yohanna Al-Hasrooni in Savary de Breve, Rome in 1613; *History of Jesus Christ* translated by Botros Makhloof, printed in Rome in 1674; *Cutting Sword*, a controversy book in Greek written by Maximoos Merghanioos (died in 1602) and translated into Arabic by Khristo Dols, Bishop of Gaza, and Bishop Yoasaf bin Suwaidan Al-Umari, printed in 1696; a book on Christian tradition, written in Greek and translated into Arabic by Deacon Safranioos of Halab Church, printed in 1740; *Eucharist*, written by Afstranioos Argents, translated by Musa'ad Nashoo, printed in Bucharest in 1747. All these translations were printed outside Lebanon in Fano in Italy, in Rome, Astana, Bucharest, etc., but all or some of them reached Lebanon to satisfy those in need of them, providing them with the necessary reasoning for the doctrinal debate which became very fierce in particular in the eighteenth century.

During that time, Mar Qazhia Monastery Press appeared; it was the first printing shop in Lebanon and the Arab East, having its letters in Syriac. The first book published by it was the *Book of Psalms* in 1610, translated into Arabic and written Karshooni style. Deacon Abdullah Al-Zakher (1680 – 1748) established Marr Yohanna Al-Sayegh Monastery Press in Al-Khenshara, near Al-Shuwair; the first book produced was *Murshid Al-Zaman wa Qestas Abadiyat Al-Insan* (Guide of Time and Balance of Man's Eternity), compiled by Jesuit Father Nairnabragh and translated by Father Botros Fromag, edited by Abdullah Zakher. This book was issued in 1733 – 1734, and most of the books from both these printing shops were related to religion. The translated books printed by Zakher include:

- *Book of Psalms*, according to the translation of Abdullah bin Al-Fadhel Al-Antaki, printed in 1735;
- *Guide of Christian*, written by Youssef Dauterman (1585 – 1652), printed in 1738;
- Guide of Wrongdoer in Secrets of Repentance and Confession, written by Father Bolos Senairi (died in 1691) in Spanish, translated into Arabic and printed in 1747;
- *Guide of Monk*, written by Father Senairi, translated by Botros Fromag and printed in 1760;
- *Clarification of Christianity*, written by one of the Paris monks, translated by Father Botros Fromag and printed in 1768. (29)

Regarding translation in the early Renaissance, it can be handled within the framework of two places:

1-   In Egypt and the Levant:

Glimpses of enlightenment appeared on the Arab Horizon in the early nineteenth century after they had led several centuries in darkness. The Arabs noticed that science is the source of power and Europe possessed material, industrial and military power thanks to the progress of science, even though Europe practised colonization and invasion, exploiting the weaknesses of nations in both Asia and Africa and imposing its hegemony over such nations to exploit their natural resources, their manpower, make them a market for its manufactured products and a field for expansion and the spreading of its political and cultural influence and languages.

Thus, it was established in the minds of Arab youth, aspiring to liberty and independence and longing for national supremacy, national dignity, self-conservation and the conservation of cultural identity, that it is incumbent upon them to resume their glorious history and seek power by pursuing the way of scientific progress, spreading education and establishing different industries.

Historical books and studies show that the period of Napoleon's Expedition to Egypt, followed by the reign of Mohammad Ali, was one of fruitful activity and great transformation. Napoleon brought with him from France a group of scientists who established a French scientific academy, schools, institutes, journals, observatories and printing shops; they studied the plants, animals, water, relief and monuments of Egypt. They established factories for paper and cloth. Then Mohammad Ali Pasha came and laid the foundations of renaissance by opening schools of military sciences, human medicine, veterinary medicine, engineering, agriculture, industries, arts and management. He issued *Al-Waqae' Al-Mesria* (Egyptian Events) and dispatched missions to study in the West.

However, it was the Arabic language which remained the language of instruction in all the governmental schools of different types and degrees for a long time.

The pioneers of this epoch knew that the first step towards scientific research is to translate modern sciences into Arabic. Therefore, they worked for the revival of translation to help modernize the territories by imparting all that is new from the West in the field of statutes, laws and knowledge, especially concerning the army, government administration and economy.

Instruction in Arabic and the need for securing its requirement for books were the main motives for translation. Establishing scientific colleges such as the College of Medicine in Al-Qaser Al-Aini in 1826 was one of the main reasons for urging translation. Within this college, its founder, Dr Claut, wrote medical books in French for the purpose of instruction; they were translated into Arabic. Dr Fijri wrote a book on botany and it was translated into Arabic; works of translation and writing came one after the other for the purpose of serving education and spreading culture in Arabic.

Men of different specializations translated books into Arabic and wrote books in Arabic. Among those men who translated and wrote in Arabic were Mohammad Ali Al-Baqli, one of the most famous surgeons of the time, Mohammad Al-Shafe'e, Ali Riyadh, Mohammad Al-Dorri, Refa'aa Al-Tahtawi in medicine, Mohammad Nada in botany and zoology, Mohammad Al-Falaki and Mohammad Al-Baiyoomi in astronomy, engineering and mathematics. They were a group who combined between authoring, translations, correction, and revision and proofreading of scientific terminology including Mohammad Omar Al-Tunisi and Ibrahim Al-Desouqi; translators at that time included Yohanna Anhoori and Youssef Far'oan.

When the British occupied Egypt in 1882, they began to change instruction from Arabic into English. This occurred in 1887, i.e. after only five years after it remained in Arabic more than sixty years. This was a regression and deterioration for Arabic, not only in Egypt, but also in all the Arab countries.

It is worth mentioning that those pioneers in the field of scientific translation laid terminology in reliance upon the old Arabic scientific books they referred to and benefited from, and relied upon the correct words contained therein. This does not mean that all the terminology used by them in authoring and translation was valid; rather, some of the terms were revised later in scientific translation and authoring and were replaced by other terms. All the efforts exerted by them came to fruition; they found a good nucleus for an Arabic scientific language of alphabet and style; they paved the way for those who came after them to follow the same track.

During that time, translation was intended to achieve some purpose. Translated books were issued as a result of being compiled from different books, and there were books having some chapters thereof left and the remaining chapters were translated. There were also books which had other parts and chapters added to them. An example of this was Refa'aa Al-Tahtawi, who was the most famous one to care about translation and to master it during that epoch in some of his books; he gathered the chapters of his book entitled *Al-Ta'arifat Al-Shafia li moridi Al-Joghrafia* (Detailed Definitions for Geography Learners) from different French books and, after translating the book, came up with a summary of these long books of science. (30)

Translation's origins did not lie in specialization; a translator used to translate books in different subjects. Sometimes a translator used to translate books in history or geography; they move to translate books in engineering, chemistry or botany. After a while, when this trend became stronger and the number of translators increased, translation tended to be specialized; for example, those who were appointed in the School of Medicine from those graduates of missions specialized in translating medical books only. Had the School of Languages remained longer, it would have laid the foundations of the rule of specialization in translation.

Moreover, the principle of participation in work was followed in keen interest in accomplishing work in as short a time as possible. More than one translator used to participate in translating a book into Arabic, especially if the book was big in size or of numerous parts.

Whereas regarding the linguistic level, a great deal of care was taken when it was noticed that there was confusion in selecting lexical items and in the wording of sentences. Revision and rephrasing were assigned to professional persons in the Arabic language such as Sheikhs of Al-Azhar. Anyhow, the style tended to acquire a scientific stamp and translators turned away from lexical restrictions and figures of speech which kept constant pressure upon Arabic prose. It was not reasonable for the translator to stick to the assonance, for example, while rendering the scientific book from French into Arabic. Thus, translation provided a great service to the Arabic language; it helped to release its shackles and included renewable meanings as well as enriched language with lots of words and structures in addition to providing a lexical work which was good for what came thereafter.

This trend in the field of translation gave something new to the field of Arabic culture and Arabic science after centuries of cultural rigidness, especially because it coincided with economical, social, scientific and educational renaissance. If such a trend had been destined to continue along the planned track, the period of pauses and degenerations, which were obstacles on the Arabs' route to the progress of civilization, would have been cut short.

However, this trend was not destined to continue; the School of Languages was cancelled after the death of Mohammad Ali; its graduates were scattered and turned into clerks in different agencies and divans. The degeneration extended throughout the reign of Abbas and Said, but the first impact of the school was not suppressed. When renaissance continued in the reign of Ismail, its students resumed their activity and returned to translation; they even wrote books and their master, Refa'aa Al-Tahtawi, returned to bear the emblem again. The tree which was planted during the reign of Mohammad Ali began to bear fruit in the reign of Ismail; however, this did not last long because of the British Occupation in 1882.

In the Levant, in the late 1800s, the US College in Beirut served Arabic language for a period of time; when established, medical education was carried out in Arabic. There were three professors who mastered Arabic and translated books of instruction into Arabic. They wrote their own books in Arabic as well; they were Fandik, Boost and Ratbat, but instruction in Arabic did not last long in this college and was changed into English.

After this experience in teaching in Arabic at the collegiate level in Al-Qaser Al-Aini and the US College in Beirut, both of which were not destined to last long, the College of Medicine in Damascus was established in 1919 to succeed them and compensate for what they had lost. It began its instruction in Arabic from its opening and has retained this until today with the several scientific colleges which were established thereafter in Syria. This is in addition to the College of Law which was established at the same time and has continued teaching in Arabic non-stop until today.

This college was established upon the decree of King Faisal I, then King of Syria, upon the ruins of the Turkish College of Medicine in Damascus which was established by a Sultanic Decree in 1901. Since its establishment, its professors have undertaken teaching in Arabic, translating and writing as well as finding the proper medical terms; they could, with efforts exerted, keep the promise and laid down valuable works in Arabic in different medical branches.

In searching for the scientific terms, professors of the college relied upon what was mentioned in the old medical books such as the Law of Avicenna, Complete Industry, Lexicology of Ibn Al-Baitar, Dawood's Notes, and modern medical books written in Egypt, the Ottoman Empire and the College of Beirut. They concluded each book with a glossary of terminology in French and Arabic; they also issued dictionaries. Among the famous doctors were Murshid Khater, Ahmad Hamdi Al-Khaiyat, Mohammad Salah Al-Din Al-Kawakebi, Michelle Al-Khoori and Hosni Sabh. The first three of those classified the Arabic version of *Clarefil Medical Multi-Lingual Dictionary* which was printed in both French and Arabic in 1955. Dr Hosni Sabh continued to occupy the position of Head of the Arabic Language Academy.

In a report about the work of translation in the College of Medicine in Damascus University, the following was mentioned: "It was only a few years and then each professor laid down his book in the branch he opted for. All professors were keen on students' continuous contact with the development of science. They set at the end of each book a dictionary for terminology in Arabic, French or English. Before long the store rooms were filled with medical books and writings full of terminology whether innovated, derived or translated. After a short while, all such terminology became in use by every layman. Rather, linguistic rules of derivation and translation were followed and chemical symbols remained in their Latin letters. Lots of words remained in their international wording which remained the same in all languages, such as hormone, vitamin, allergy and gangrene. Some words, which were taken by the Westerners from us or which we took from the Westerners, such as syrup, catheter, asthma, etc., were returned to the Arabic words. However, we reused lots of the old words which express the meaning intended from them, such as ashawa, bala, jadra, safal, sehaf, amlaqa, usaida, etc.

Those professors and their followers helped give more prestige to the Arabic language; they knew its characteristics and probed its inner essence, thus coming up with its pearls and spreading them in their works and translations. Since its establishment, the College of Medicine has continued to graduate doctors in Arabic at the same level as any college in the Arab Homeland and indeed the world. Having laid foundations, its footsteps were followed by other scientific colleges established in Syria.

This experience in teaching in Arabic was destined to continue and succeed, and one of the benefits was to have professors, books and methodologies for translating the current education in other countries.

2-   In Other Arab Countries:

At times when endeavours were made in Egypt and the Levant for translation – translation of instruction and translation of departments and institutions as well as the development of the Arabic language through translation from other foreign languages – there were endeavours in other Arab countries to struggle against foreignization, to stick to the Arabic language and to maintain its existence.

Among the results of the French invasion of Algeria in 1830 and the following imposition of French hegemony in Algeria, Tunisia and Morocco, was the sticking of the French to the policy of merging and franchising in the Arab Maghreb in general: Algeria, Tunisia and Morocco. However, there were different methods for meeting the aim, i.e. to create a generation away from its national language and culture. It is a disconnection, imposed by the colonizer between the present of the Arab nation in this region and its past, in order to get such a nation to forget its national identity and cause it to lose its relationship with its heritage to adopt a culture alien to its own culture and speak in a language different from its own language: French language and culture.

However, sticking to the Arabic language was part and parcel of the insistence upon land, liberty and independence. Therefore, it was one of the factors which enhanced the roots of the national struggle to abort the attempts at colonization and clearly show national identity and self-preservation.

In Tunisia, Al-Zaitoona University and both the Al-Sadeqiya and Al-Khaldouniya schools were citadels for religion and the Arabic language. Their men, including professors and students, expressed their stance for protecting Arab heritage and helping Tunisian people to get rid of cultural dependency. Methods of resisting franchising were various, including claim for reform for Al-Zaitoona programme to keep up with the age and modern school; establishing national cultural societies such as Khaldoon Society, Ancient Sadiqiya Society, which were concerned with spreading among the youth the principles of modern sciences in Arabic; opening free contemporary schools to teach in Arabic. In the 1940s, translated scientific lessons were included in Zaitoona education without the permission of the supervisory authority therein, and arithmetics, algebra, geometry, physics and chemistry were taught within the lessons of Zaitoona University, and scientific scholastic books were written. The National Movement sponsored this tendency. This forced the colonization authorities to generalize the programmes of Al-Sadeqiya School by opening parallel sections to them in several secondary institutes even in Karno School, the citadel of French instruction.

However, this trend of translation lacked accurate planning because the circumstances in which it occurred were those of national struggle for liberation from colonial dependency.

With the beginning of independence, the Arabic language was considered the language of the country in the constitution and consequently the language of instruction. However, lacking the competent educational entity capable of providing instruction in Arabic caused teaching in the language to move slowly. After that, primary education was translated and the scope of education was widened in secondary schools and universities, especially in colleges of arts and human sciences.

Morocco, however, which had spent forty years under French protection, conserved Arabic in its land despite the efforts of the foreign authorities to impose the French language in the institutes of administration and education. Al-Qarawieen University, having its glorious past in spreading science and knowledge and allowed for studying contemporary sciences in Arabic, persevered as well. Then, primary and secondary schools, which provide sciences in Arabic, were established.

After independence, Morocco set a plan for reforming education based upon totally generalizing primary education and partially generalizing secondary education and higher education in the field of arts, law and social sciences. Steps were completed according to the availability of teaching staff able to teach scientific and technical subjects in Arabic.

Algeria was exposed to a fierce settler colonization, lasting for one hundred and thirty years, and practising a policy based upon spreading poverty and ignorance, erasing Algerian identity and changing geographical, cultural and civilization Algerian belonging. However, resistance was always a constant activity against such policy, and cultured persons, sticking to originality and national societies which were constituted in Algeria, encountered the plans of the colonizer.

After the victory of the Revolution and Independence in 1962, sincere efforts were exerted in spreading education and translating it. It was mentioned in the National Charter: "The choice between National Language and foreign language is not available and is irrevocable. There shall be no discussion about translation from now on except in relation to the content, medium, methodology and stages...." Algeria is moving ahead in translating science in its different stages and is seriously seeking to satisfy the needs for the same, including teachers, authored or translated books.

Reference should be made to the efforts which have been exerted and are still being exerted in the other Arab countries; the Italian colonization in Libya tried to impose its language by force to annex the territories to its empire. However, after the decline of its hegemony and Arab Jamahiriya making education in Arabic and also in theoretical university colleges; however, in the main colleges of applied sciences, they still retain English as the language of instruction in expectation for securing the requirements of translation thereof, namely, competent teachers, books and scientific references. The State established the Arab Development Institute and Jihad Libyans' Center for Historical Studies, and both were concerned with translation and authoring in addition to other objectives.

In other countries, such as Sudan, Jordan, the Kingdom of Saudi Arabia, Kuwait and all the rest of the Gulf Countries, sincere efforts are exerted to spread and translate education, and their public education is in Arabic. In addition, teaching in colleges of arts and human sciences is also in Arabic. The difficulty in the scope of teaching lies in the technical and scientific colleges, as efforts are made in this regard to satisfy the requirements including teachers and books.

Translating books of higher education is not just a matter of making a decision, even though decisions are the main starting point; rather, it is difficult, constructive and hard work, requiring competent human power, a valid educational medium and unification of terms and translation of books, scientific studies and researches. However, at the national and Pan-Arab levels, making such a decision is so important and necessary that any effort exerted and every sacrifice provided is found agreeable.

Each step taken by an Arab country in translating education, especially university education, necessitates attention being given to translating methodological books, scientific cultural reference books and, most importantly, researches and studies bearing the latest information acquired by science and technology so as to make them accessible to teachers and students.

This does not mean that there is no translation when higher education is provided in a foreign language; rather, it becomes narrow and is not benefited from, except by a limited number who are willing to follow up what is new with others or access foreign literary masterpieces in Arabic.

Transliteration and translation run parallel to one another: the former is a process of origination and the latter is one of modernization, and both are complementary to each other.

1.2: Most Important Schools of Translation

Throughout successive epochs, the world witnessed famous schools of translation art; such schools greatly influenced the neighbouring civilizations and played a major role in conveying the cultures, thoughts and heritage of nations into other languages. The most important of these schools are as follows:

First: School of Alexandria (306 BC):

The School of Alexandria was concerned with studying medicine in addition to theology. Lectures and explanations were given for sixteen of Galenus' books. In addition, the School of Alexandria was more concerned than others with the researches into chemistry and astronomy, to the extent that when the Arab Islamic Conquest came, Alexandria was famous for the scientific trend in its studies; it is the original place of Modern Platonism.

Max Mayerhoaf lists a number of philosophers and physicians who graduated from the School of Alexandria in the sixth and seventh centuries (AD) including for example: Yahia Al-Nahawi, Astafan Aliskandari, Yohanna Al-Afami and Sergeoos Al-Raasa'ani; he considered that the writing of those had played an important role in the early studies of the Arabs.

If we move to the region near the Arab Peninsula, across its expansions distributed everywhere, we find that all the places where Greek sciences prospered were the ones where their inhabitants spoke middle Persian and Syriac, such as Al-Raha, Nusaibeen, Qansareen, Jandesapur in relation to Al-Nasatera, Antakia and Amed (Diar Baker) in relation to Al-Ya'aqeba. This is in addition to the fact that there were some schools in monasteries. It is noted that the general character distinguishing these schools was that they were primarily theological in addition to teaching secular sciences such as grammar, philosophy, medicine, music, mathematics and astronomy. As distinct from the studies made in this regard, philosophical education was limited to an aspect of Aristotelian logic, whereas the medical education was limited to the great books of Hippocrates and Galenus. Greek was taught in addition to Syriac in such schools. This did not prevent some translations being made from Greek into Syriac for different purposes.

Second: School of Qansareen:

Located on the bank of Euphrates River, in this school, competent and outstanding scientists appeared, making their impact upon the development of Arab scientific thinking. They were the first to translate philosophical and medical books from Greek into Syriac; perhaps Saweera Sawbokht (died in 667 AD), student of Yaqoob Al-Rahawi (died in 708 AD) and Marjerjis Bishop of Arabs (died in 725 AD) were the most skilful scientists of this school.

Third: School of Jundesapur (500 AD):

This was established by the King of Persia, Khesro Anoshrowan, who allowed the Greek philosophers to have asylum in his country when they were expelled by the Byzantine Emperor Justinian who closed their school in Athens. This institution, which was sponsored by the King of Persia, was characterized by the fact that it was not limited to Greek, Syriac and Persian studies; rather, it was oriented towards the philosophy and sciences of India where a great deal of it was translated into the Fahlawia language. It contained the greatest medical temple, to which a hospital, headed by Georgeoos bin Bukhteshiou', the physician of Abbassides, was annexed. Greek medicine and Indian medicine were taught and developed in this school. Students of this school included the Arabian physician, Al-Hareth bin Kelda, and his son, Al-Nadher. Al-Razi mentioned Shenaq, writer of *Treatise on Poisons*, which was translated by Manca into Persian. In the First Abbasid Era, physicians of this school moved to Baghdad and most of them were among the household of Bukhteshiou'; from this family came physicians and ministers of caliphs and from them came the physicians of hospitals and teachers of medicine and philosophy.

Fourth: School of Haran:

This school was established in the era of Alexander and continued for a long time as a centre for National Greek studies and the study of New Platonism. It was a centre for apostatizers whose language was Syriac. Most of the concerns of this school were focused upon mathematics, astronomy and astrology. The most famous scientists of this school were Thabet bin Qurra and his son, Senan bin Thabet, and Al-Batani, the astronomer and mathematician. It had an effective impact in spreading mathematics and astronomy.

Fifth: School of Al-Raha:

De Poore says, "The style of Al-Raha became so elegant that it was good to be used in writing. It is known that the language taught was Syriac and Greek. It was closed by Emperor Zinon because its masters were Nastooris in their opinions. They escaped to Nusaibin.

Sixth: School of Nusaiabin:

The masters of this school, being Nastooris, defended their religious beliefs supporting their trends by theories derived from the philosophy of Greek. Therefore, Modern Platonism prospered and extended to Persia; in their defence of religion, they were defending Greek philosophy.

Seventh: School of Qesaria:
It was established by Origence who left the School of Alexandria, which was similar to the latter.

Eighth: School of Antakia:
This was founded by Malikhon in about 270 AD. Modern Platonism flourished in it; this school is characterized by derivational specialization from Greek into Syriac.

It is clear from all of this that, for these countries, the epoch between the emergence of the Christian sects and Arabs' conquest was rich in translation from Greek into Syriac as well as in interpretations and explanations; this was due to the fact that Greek philosophy supported these groups in explaining and supporting their beliefs.

It can be said that such schools were a fertile soil for receiving the seeds of Arab thought which was about to emerge and appear. However, the role of such schools was limited to conserving this environment in which mental and intellectual activity was alive; they did not produce philosophers or scientists with outstanding gifts or books or researches of eternal value.

These schools provided the foundations upon which the Arab Muslims could base religious, medical and mathematical philosophy and sciences and to absorb from it deeply-rooted prosperous sciences. (31)

1.3: Types of Translation

The trend of translation was and remains the cornerstone in each cultural renaissance and the means for attaining goals, achieving objectives and transcending reality.

This trend has been active, for a while, during the last period, and encountered problems at another time, and moved from Egypt to the Levant, then to the other Arabian countries. It is still in constant development and expansion today, even though it requires more support, encouragement, coordination and planning so as to fulfil its role and attain its objective.

Currently, there is a differentiation between two distinct types of translation, namely:

First: Oral Instant Translation:
This is the translation which is made orally in fulfilment of the needs of understanding between the speakers of two different languages. It is of old origin and people have needed it for a long time. It has become a craft

or independent specialization at the present time. It has its own institutes, programmes, foundations and techniques, where those willing have it as a hobby and only those outstanding can master it having only the original talent and good training and practice.

Second: Written Translation:
   This involves translating written text into another written text; this translation is supposed to be more accurate and better than oral instant translation. This is because its tools are the pen and paper which pave the way for more deliberation and accuracy.

1.3.1: First Requirement: First Opinion of Researchers in Branches of Translation

   The view of researchers is that written translation is divided into two branches:

1- Administrative and Media Translation:
   This translation is part of the work of some departments, administrations and institutions; it is concerned with conveying news and articles to the mass media. Political, commercial, banking and press translation are similar to it.

2- Cultural Translation:
   This is the translation of intellectual, scientific, literary and artistic works from one language into another.
   This type of translation is very important and effective because it is the means of cultural interchange between nations and peoples and the means for scientific progress and knowledge enrichment. Consequently, it is one of the pillars of economic and social development and the building of national prosperous civilization.
   Cultural translation is made in the Arab Homeland from foreign languages into the Arabic language, or vice versa, from Arabic into foreign languages. This was termed as "Arabicization" in the first case and "foreignization" in the second case. This cultural translation is divided into two parts: scientific and literary translation.

(A)   Scientific Translation:
   Scientific translation refers to the translation of books of basic science, such as books of mathematics, physics, chemistry and biology, geology, botany and zoology, and books of applied sciences: medicine, dentistry,

pharmacology, nursing and engineering sciences, with all their branches, and different technical sciences.

The translator of scientific works should master Arabic and the foreign source language, as is the case with any translator in general. A translator must be specialized in the scientific subject to be translated. In other words, medicine should be translated only by a doctor, and books in chemistry should be translated only by a chemist.

If a good scientific translation is required, it must be done by persons specialized in the same field, provided that such a specialized person has an inclination to this scientific activity, has powerful language and good expression and output.

This is not strange; the scope of each field of science has become so wide, and its terminology has become so diverse, that it can be understood only by a person specialized in that science. It is natural that a scientific or technical translation be done by a person having full command of it.

Dr Mohammad Awadh Mohammad says that in order that a technical, i.e. cultural and scientific translation, be a successful and fruitful work and useful cultural activity, a translator must have full power in linguistic and technical aspects. A linguistic composition varies according to the variety of languages; it also varies according to the variety of scientific or literary materials handled by books or articles and researches.

As for social and human sciences, in addition to the previous conditions to be met in translating scientific and technical books, they need good phrasing and style to attract the readers and satisfy their linguistic taste and cause the reader to like the translated book.

Under this title come the books of philosophy, sociology, demography, education, psychology, history, geography, economics, law, politics and linguistics.

Some researchers take the view that a scientific translation is the easiest type of translation if undertaken by a person experienced in the material to be translated and the corresponding terminology. A translator shall remember to render the required meaning without any confusion, to select proper words capable of expression and to acceptably phrase their style in an easy and proper Arabic language without complication or affectation.

Scientific translation requires that scientific researches and studies also be translated, not only books and publications, because such researches and studies represent new developments in the field of science and bear the ideas, opinions, experiences and experiments of scientists who work in universities, research centres and scientific laboratories in developed countries.

(B)   Literary Translation:

A literary translation is that of literary books and publications such as novels, stories, plays, poetry, articles and studies of an artistic nature. Books on history of literature and literary criticism, however, lie in the centre position between arts on one hand and social and human science on the other, in terms of subject and style.

Most of those having knowledge of the problems of translation and those who suffered from rendering and experienced both its hard and easy conditions of work believe that literary translation is more difficult than scientific translation. This is due to the fact that a literary text is not merely an idea or ideas only; rather, it relies upon the feelings and imagination of an author; it is a text woven by a talented poet or prose writer intending it to be exciting and charming.

Dr Mohammad Awadh Mohammad says, The first condition to be met by a translator intending to translate a literary work emulating the translated work is that a translator should be himself a man of letters. It is not enough for a translator to have full command of both languages; literature is a spirit, tendency and natural disposition and all these are things relying upon a nature within one's self and are not acquired by study or memorization only. If we require from a person translating a book in medicine to be a doctor, it is no wonder that a person translating literature shall be a man of letters or translating poetry to be a poet.

Some researchers see that there are differences between the translation of literary and scientific texts:

1- A literary text is not changed with the lapse of time, i.e. it keeps its literary value though it is related to a certain environment and age. We read today the lines of Abu Al-Alaa Al-Ma'arri's fixed rhyme poems, the plays of Shakespeare and other works of Eastern and Western literature, not in the way we read a text addressing people who merely died long ago, but we read them as texts appealing to the ideas, feelings and imaginations in a similar manner to those aroused by literary texts whose writing ink has not dried yet. Scientific texts, however, lose their scientific nature and keep their historical value with the development of science; they represent what is attained by the human mind in the field of science at that particular point in time.

2- A scientific text, when rendered, needs only an accurate term and clear phrasing to give it proper meaning, whereas a literary text needs a selected word and good phrasing. Therefore, knowledge alone is not enough in literary translation; rather, a foreign taste and true talent should be available.

Beautiful words and expressions should be translated into equivalent beautiful words and expressions; the feeling experienced by a person reading the source text has to be experienced by a person reading the text when translated. (32) However, does the translation become totally equivalent to the original? Perhaps it does, but this is difficult. There is an Italian proverb which claims that translation is disloyalty, i.e. whatever effort is exerted in translation, it can not reach the level of the source text. However, there is no alternative to translating literary works because they, alone among the arts, have language as their medium; music, sculpture and painting have no language; rather, translation is the language of all people, but literature is not comprehensible except through language and its masterpieces exist in all languages.

The field of competition, skill and creativity in literary translation is very vast without a known destination. The maximum aim to be aspired to is to have a target text equivalent to the source text in terms of beauty and charm until it becomes a literary work in itself in Arabic, not just an echo of a foreign work.

Hafiz Ibrahim, describing a translated work, says, A source and target text came as a beautiful lady having her reflection in the mirror in terms of similarity and identity and this is what is desirable in a literary translation.

This leads us to say that whoever wants to translate literature must himself be a man of letters; literature is a natural disposition; honesty should be his driver; inner taste should be his guide and professionalism should be his objective.

If this applies to literature in general, it applies even more to poetry because poetry has more different arts in terms of tone, suggestion and symbol than prose literature. Al-Jahiz was aware of this fact; he said, "Poetry can not be translated nor rendered; whenever it is transformed, its form and charm are lost and become unfamiliar." (33)

1.3.2: Second Requirement: Second Opinion of Researchers in Branches of Translation

Other researchers see that translation can be divided into several types other than those stated by former researchers. They illustrate this by saying that if we examine a certain stage such as the Abbasid Era to see what types of translation exist, we will see the following:

1- Literary Translation:

Literary translation means to put a word instead of another word where we do not consider cohesion and coherence. This method was selected by Yohanna bin Al-Batreeq and Abdul-Masih bin Al-Na'ema Al-Hemsi, etc. It is an improper method of translation for several reasons:

1- It does not keep cohesion among the parts of the sentence; it is known that this lack of cohesion among the parts of a sentence destroys meaning and even gives an opposite meaning at other times.

2- Sometimes language does not have an equivalent for the source word and thus the translator needs to put the source word as it is in the target text.

3- Figures of speech cannot be literally translated; rather, a translator should express their meaning irrespective of the number of words, their length or shortness. If a person tries to translate literally, it is natural to make a mistake in rendering meaning.

4- Styles differ from one language to another; an Arab person writes in a style different, or even opposite at times, from that of an Indian. Writing in the language and style of another language ought to be clear to be bad and proper.

2- Literary Translation:

In literary translation or semantic translation, a translator produces a sentence expressing the meaning of the source sentence without regard to the equivalence in the number of words, length or shortness; what is required here is to express meaning in any manner. In this method, a translator considers the style of the target language. This type of language is very good. Dr Omar Farroukh says, This (semantic translation) means that a translator reads the sentence and assimilates its meaning in his mind then expresses it in the other language using a sentence having the same meaning whether both sentences have the same number of words or not.

3- Free Translation:

The third type of translation which was common in the Abbasid Era was free translation; this means that a translator reads the source text without considering the number of words but renders the meaning in the words and expressions of the target language. This also requires clarification in a place facilitating for the reader to understand it in the target text not outside it. Scholar Shibli Al-No'amani Al-Hindi says, Caliph Al-Ma'moun used to search for translators who have the upper

hand in the subject so as to solve the original problems of translation; this
type of translators included Hunain bin Isshaq and Yaqoub Al-Kanadi.

4- Summary Translation:
This means that a translator reads a paragraph of the source text and
does not consider the words but considers the meaning required then
expresses the meaning in short terms, so that he can produce a summarized
book out of the source text. We can call this translation Extractive
Translation. As Dr Omar Farroukh said in this regard, "Authored books
are attributed to translators but it is better to handle all the product of
translators, whether it is said to be authoring or translation, as being
translation because any product claimed by translator to have been their
own ideas is extracted from the books they previously translated."
This is another term for summary translation and we can not give it
another name.

5- Anatomical Translation:
In this category, a translator translates the text then adds explanation
and clarification where needed; he adds something and removes something
so that a text can be clear for the reader who can not unravel confusion.
German Orientalist Zigrid Honka said, Hunain bin Isshaq had a vast
knowledge; he was a master of the material he was translating, adding to
points of weakness or confusion from his own knowledge to make them
clear and giving an explanatory introduction.

6- Direct Translation:
Direct translation or oral translation means that a translator reads the
text then simultaneously translates it. This type of translation is difficult
and can not be done without training for this process or without being
professional in this art as well as in both the source and target language.
There were people who used to translate in this way. Zigrid Honka says, A
delegation from India came to Abi Jaafar Al-Mansour in 154 Hijri and had
among it a man skilful in understanding the movements of planets, their
calculations and all the works of astronomy according to the teachings of
the scientists of his nation, especially according to the approach of a book
in Sanskrit entitled *Brahamsebah Tasdehant*, written in 628 Hijri or (6 or
7) by the astronomer and mathematician Brahamakt; Al-Mansour asked
this Indian man to state the summary of this book.
Oral translation is nothing but this type.

7- Beneficial Translation:

This means that a translator puts the source in front of him then prepares a book benefiting from it. The process can also be called "Selective Translation"; the writer selects texts from books and produces another book out of such selected texts and signs it in his name. This type of translation was known in the Abbasid Era. Dr Ahmad Amin says:

The Persians made a major contribution to literature; their writing of stories, such as Kalila and Dimna ,which were translated from Persian into Arabic, were one foundation upon which the subsequent generations based the Arab stories that we have today. Ibn Al-Nadeem narrates that Mohammad bin Abdoos Al-Jahishawi, writer of the book entitled *Ministers* started writing a book in which he selected thousand night pleasant conversations of the Arabs, non-Arabs and Romans, each independent and not attached to each other. He brought travellers and took from them the best they knew and selected from the books written about pleasant night conversations and myths as well as whatever he liked. He was a virtuous man and therefore he gathered from this about 408 nights; each night contained a pleasant night conversation consisting of 50 pages, more or less. Then, he abruptly died before achieving his ambition to complete 1000 pleasant night chats.

8- Analytical Translation:

An analytical translation means that a translator translates a text then analyzes where its meaning is clear and its problems are solved. Those types of translators included Yaqoub Al-Kanadi, Philosopher of Islam, about whom the Scholar Shibli Al-No'amani Al-Hindi says, "He was proficient in Greek in addition to Greek, Persian and Sanskrit sciences. He translated books of philosophy and solved the problems in the original text."

9- Natural Translation:

A natural translation means that a source book is translated and phrased in a linguistic frame so that nobody can feel it is a translated text. Isshaq Hunain was one of the most professional persons to use this type of translation. Zigrid Honka says, "The man (Hunain) went through the way of glory as well in another field, i.e. translation, until he outdid Masawaih himself. Sons of Moosa admired the man and his talents. He was the genius to be relied upon; in his translation, he does not replace a word for a word, but accurately and artfully gives the equivalent meaning in an Arab wording.

10- Universal Translation:

This means that a translator takes several copies of one book then makes a complete version out of them, combining the different aspects from all versions. Then, the translator adds to it what was included in different other versions and finally translates it into his own language. This can be called a preparatory translation. Orientalist Carl Proclman says about Buhram bin Marawan Shah and Moosa bin Easa Al-Kasrawi:

"They both brought several versions of the book entitled *Khadaynamak* and took out an edited text according to their approach in criticism, but they handled the original book text by making changes and alterations and added to it from other Persian sources."

11- Arabicization:

Arabicization, Indicization or Persicization is a process in translation in which a translator phrases the word in Arabic, Indian or Persian wording, i.e. making it easy for the reader to read and articulate it, and this is acceptable. Moreover, it is common among the translations of such languages and an evidence of their life. Writers of the book entitled *Scientific Translation* say:

"Arabicization is inevitable in translation among living languages; this process does not depreciate a language but it is common and acceptable among languages."

Dr Hamid Taher says: "It is acceptable to put the foreign word or phrase as it is in its place and indicate that it is difficult with an Arab suggestion deemed fit by the translator."

This also applies to names as it applies to words. Dr Ahmad Amin says about Hunain, If Hunain finds it ineviable, he uses scientific terms in their wording such as *doghmatikin, physiologia and pathologia*. This occurs with names and is what we call Arabicization.

12- False Translation:

This type of translation is something by which the Abbassi Era was characterized; rather, it was a result of numerous translations done during that era and the profits it used to yield. When translators felt that caliphs and princes were concerned with translation, they started to translate a chapter of a book and call it a book, make some alterations in it and make it in a translated book announcing that it is a translated book, or translate a chapter from a book already written and attribute it to another author. For example, *Kitab Al-Rawabi'* (Book of Springs) was attributed to Plato; *Kitab Al-Tiffaha* (Book of Apple), *Kitab Al-Robobiya* (Book of Godhood), *Kitab Al-Idah fi Al-Khair Al-Mahdh* (Book of Clarification in Pure Good) and *Kitab Ser Al-Asrar* (Book of Secret of Secrets). All these books were attributed to Aristotle while the original and true writer is unknown. Moreover, the second book might have been a translation of Fidoan's discourse by Plato; the third book was excerpts from *Nines of Plato*; the fourth book was a text derived from the book entitled *Divinities* for Aprocles, while the fifth book, Ser Al-Asrar, was written by an anonymous author.

Hence, one of the researchers wondered, saying, "What is the motive for this plagiarizing? What reasons lie behind it?" He answers this question, saying that there are three reasons for this as follows:

1- A keen interest in earning money: When caliphs and ministers began to pay generously for translation, the keen interest in earning money became greater in the hearts of unjust translators. They translated a given chapter from a book and called it a book. Dr Omar Farroukh says: "Translators were so greedy that they were keenly interested in earning money through translation; they used to translate a chapter from a book and call it a book, make slight alterations in a translated book and then sell it saying it is new, or attribute a book to a person other than its genuine writer (as they did with the book entitled *Othology*; they attributed it to Aristotle while it was extracted from a book by Plato).

2- Scholars and scientists took pride in having the books of great people: Some scientists and scholars took pride in gathering books of great people including philosophers and intellectuals, which were not in the possession of others.

3- Error of attribution to a person other than the author: Some scientists made mistakes in attributing work to the genuine and original writer. A manuscript contained parts which a person was accustomed to ones similar to it and he thought it was done by him. Such plagiarizations took place in books of chemistry and magic.

This researcher sees that when reading these words, some can make the mistake of doubting the works translated in the Abbassi Era. Translators used techniques of criticism that made them sure of the book they wanted to translate. These techniques included:

1- They searched for the style selected by the author of a book; if they found it differed from his style, they accused him of plagiarizing it. For example, when Hunain bin Isshaq compared the style of the book entitled *Al-Kabir fi Al-Nabdh* (Great in Pulsing) to the style of Galenus and his scientific level, he judged that the book was mistakenly attributed to Galenus.

2- They searched for unity of ideas; the ideas shown in *Kitab Al-Tiffaha* (Book of Apple), *Kitab Al-Robobiya* (Book of Godhood), *Kitab Al-Idah* (Book of Clarification) and *Kitab Ser Al-Asrar* (Secret of Secrets) were not suitable to what Aristotle talked about and thus they were proven to have been plagiarized.

3- They gathered several copies of one book. If they compared one copy to the other, support and confirmation was given that it was genuine. No doubt the number of similar or different copies of a book aroused trust or doubt in the book attributed to the author. (34)

Simultaneous Interpretation:

In the modern age, with the spread of mass media, increasing travel among countries, growing numbers of tourists and visitors, easy travel from one place to another and spread of business, it has become common to use simultaneous translation. This type of translation is defined by Shehada Al-Khoori as "A translation which is made orally in fulfilment of the needs to achieve understanding among people speaking different languages; it is a specialization mastered by a few people."

Simultaneous interpretation is more difficult than oral translation because it is the only one relying upon the translator's use of the sense of hearing, while other types of translation rely upon the use of sight, hearing, touch or both of them at least.

A simultaneous interpretation requires mastery of two linguistic systems between which translation is made unilaterally or bilaterally. The most important factors of success for it include:

- Maximum knowledge of both language systems;
- Rich cultural background;
- Constant follow-up of events of the hour;
- Active memory span as a result of reading and reviewing all mass media;
- Quick wit and good action when encountering certain difficulties;
- Proper words in the foreign language;
- A translator should be bold and fluent in language;
- A translator should be deliberate and quick at the same time;
- Trying to be intuitive and anticipating what the speaker will say;
- Keeping in good health, having a balanced diet and taking sufficient rest before undertaking a simultaneous interpretation job because it needs as much concentration as possible.

Translation Act Theory:

In 1984 German researcher, Holes Mantari, developed **Translation Act** theory after several centuries over which translation witnessed different theories and orientations in which a translator was enslaved for the good of a source text or the original writer is enslaved for the good of the reader. Mantari's theory reviews a new functionally-oriented theory in theoretical and scientific translation. In the light of this theory, translation becomes a process of communication among cultures, as a result of which a text is produced, able to accurately perform certain functions within a certain context. This theory does not allow a real importance for an approach between the source and target texts or for linguistic considerations. Rather, it puts translation within a wider context for cooperative communication among professional translators and customers requiring translation.

When Mantari presented her theory, she took into consideration providing a theoretical foundation and conceptual system resulting in an approach that can be followed by professional translators. For the sake of developing this theory, Mantari focused on the theory of communication and the theory of action. The former is used to determine the contents of a communication process across the borders of cultures, while the theory of action helps her prescribe the certain characteristics for a translation act.

Third Requirement: Translation Tools:

Translation requires several tools so that a translation work can be produced in a distinct fashion from all aspects. The more these tools are excellent and wonderful, the nearer they are to perfection. Adding such features which a translator should have, including delicacy, mastery of both languages, great accuracy and high attention span, are factors helping a translator to perform his work, such as general and specialized dictionaries.

Translation is a hard art requiring talent developed by improvement and training; it is an appreciation of both the source language and target language. Moreover, translation helps a translator to be patient, tactful, accurate in expression, judgment and selection of proper words, which is very difficult. It sometimes means that a translator has to learn how to achieve understanding and taste in words which were not found by the Arabs, how to translate a proverb or a saying having no equivalent in Arabic; thus, he is forced to transliterate and adapt it to the standard Arabic language.

Researchers see that transliterating translators who existed in the First Abbasid Era knew Arabic in addition to the languages they used to translate from. They relied upon memorization and volumes in using the lexical repertoire of the foreign language they used to translate from. It was not possible for them to have a Greek-Arabic dictionary, Farsi-Arabic dictionary or Syriac-Arabic dictionary available. A translator used to make an effort to select the translated word according to his understanding, taste and ability to comprehend the meaning intended as well as his ability in Arabic itself, especially in derivation and conjugations thereof.

The trend of translation was greatly active in the early twentieth century; members of scientific missions, dispatched by governments abroad, especially France, began to return to their countries and occupy scientific and cultural positions in the State as well as being assigned to translate books of science in which they specialized.

Arabic dictionaries are the tools to be used by a translator in addition to foreign Arabic dictionaries and vice versa. These dictionaries were necessary for the trend of translation. After the emergence of printing shops, orientalists began to lay down foreign Arabic dictionaries. In 1632, Gegows Arabic-Latin Dictionary was printed in Milano City in Italy in four volumes. Then, after twenty years, Yoleus Indian Dictionary (1596 – 1667) was published. This orientalist was a student for Irbaneus, originator of Leaden Arab Press in Holland, and the intellectual relationship between Arabic and Latin was an incentive for the emergence of a group of Latin dictionaries. Thus, Maninski Polish Dictionary was published in five languages: Arabic, Farsi, Turkish, German and Latin; moreover, Fretagh's German Dictionary was published between 1788 and 1861 and is an Arabic-Latin Dictionary.

Arab translators from French into Arabic relied in the first two thirds of the nineteenth century upon Herban Dictionary (1783 - 1806) French Arabic and vice versa. They also relied upon Kazmeriski Arabic-French Dictionary, which was printed in Paris in 1860 and upon Sharbono Arabic-French Dictionary.

During these days, translation was focused upon rendering from French into Arabic; this is because the missions were then being dispatched to France. When the US College was established in Beirut, English began to compete with French, and concern began to be given to English. Its American and British professors were the first pioneers in providing sciences from English into Arabic, and they were joined in this effort by their students, such as Dr Yaqoub Sarrouf.

Since the second half of the nineteenth century, French and English have shared the translation trend, and it was natural for English-Arabic dictionaries to successively appear.

Orientalists began this activity; Badger issued his English Arabic Dictionary in 1881. In 1884, the Dictionary of Shtingas (of German origin, English residence and death), an English-Arabic dictionary, appeared. Then, Sucrate Spiro English-Arabic Dictionary was published and was printed by Al-Moqattam Press in 1897; Dictionary Hanna Abkarious (of Armenian origin) was published in 1877; Dictionary of Harvi Porter was published and printed by Al-Moqattam Press in 1895, followed by Wortabet, then Dictionary of Ibrahim was issued in English-Arabic in 1905, and finally Elias Anton Elias issued an English-Arabic dictionary in 1913 which continued to increase its editions and was followed with an Arabic-English dictionary.

After that Ismail Mazhar came and issued a valuable English-Arabic dictionary; Ismail Mazhar was not only a translator but was also a scholar who laid down new terminology for words never known by the Arabs, and perhaps this dictionary is the nearest one to standard language.

Regarding Italian-Arabic dictionaries, a dictionary was published for Monk Rophael Zakhoor, of Hallabi origin, born in Egypt, then a dictionary for Riyadh Jaiyed which was called *Italian-Arabic Dictionary*.

In the case of German-Arabic dictionaries, Adolph & Hormond Arabic-German Dictionary was issued and in 1960 the German-Arabic Technical Dictionary was issued by Egyptian engineer, Wadee' Fanoos.

There is no doubt that these dictionaries are indispensable tools for a translator; moreover, they are also indispensable in the fields of sciences, especially in the case of dictionaries issued by specialized scientists in addition to dictionaries published by specialized organizations, agencies and institutions in their work field, such as the *Unified Medical Dictionary* which was produced by the World Health Organization. Specialized dictionaries in Arab countries include the Dictionary of Dr Ahmad Bek Easa in botany and agriculture, entitled the *Dictionary of Plants' Names*; it is one in which the lexicographer handled the scientific names of plants and mentioned their equivalents in Arabic, and then mentioned under the Latin scientific name the species to which each plant belongs, its name in French and English. This dictionary was printed in 1930, and the *Dictionary of Agricultural Terms* in French by Prince Mustafa Al-Shehabi.

There are also dictionaries in medicine, such as the English-Arabic *Medical Dictionary* by Dr Ibrahim Mansour, which was printed in Egypt in 1891; the French-Arabic *Medical Dictionary* by Dr Mahmoud Roshdi Al-Baqli, one of the members of the educational mission to Paris; it was printed in Paris in 1870; the *Medical Scientific Dictionary* in Arabic and French by Na'ama Iskandar, which was printed in Alexandria in 1893, and the English-Arabic *Dictionary of Medical Sciences* by Dr Mohammad Sharaf, printed in Cairo in 1927.

There is also a valuable Arabic-French-English dictionary of animals by Amin Al-Maaloouf, in which the Arabic for the animal is added to it.

Al-Maalouf also has a small valuable dictionary in astronomy in English and Arabic.

It is recommended that translators refer to the English-Arabic *Dictionary of Civilization Terms*, by Dr Magdi Wahba, published in 1973.

A translator from English can refer to dictionaries of words such as the *Dictionary of Idiomatic Words and Expressions*, issued by Ismail Mazhar in 1950. Moreover, there are also countless dictionaries in foreign languages in sciences and arts, language, associations; the best dictionaries to be referred are the *Oxford Dictionary*, *Webster's Dictionary* and, in French, the different Larousse dictionaries. This is in addition to English Encyclopedia, Great French Encyclopedia and US Encyclopedia. If a translator is translating Islamic texts, he should refer to Islamic encyclopaedias and the like.

A translator can make great use of the footnotes and commentaries at the end of translated scientific books and diligences to which translators were guided; most of them are people of science. A translator should also make great use of the terms laid down by the Egyptian Academy of Language in Arts and Literature.

A translator should also, especially in the field of literary translation, be addicted to reading Arabic literature books, such as the books of Al-Jahiz, Abi Al-Faraj Al-Asfahani and Abi Hayan Al-Tawhidi of the old era, and Al-Mazeni, Ahmad Hassan Al-Zayat, Al-Manfalooti, Taha Hussain and Al-Aqqad from the modern era.

1.4: Effects of Translation

Islam urged the seeking of knowledge and science from anywhere and urged that full use be made of the wisdom available to civilizations and nations in different spots of the world, as long as this achieves benefit for Islam and Muslims. The results of this were that the Greek, Persian and Indian thinking were translated into Arabic, the language of Islam and Muslims. One of the researchers believes that this translation had positive as well as negative impacts. Positive impacts of translation include the following:

1- Preserving Greek, Indian and Persian heritage, especially, as beneficial for other nations.

2- Improving this heritage and indicating the shortcomings in it through revision and criticism.

3- Establishing a glorious Islamic civilization combining traditional and intellectual sciences after passing by the stages of receiving and contemplation, thus causing it to acquire a permanent nature, distinct from previous and subsequent civilizations.

4- The emergence of a large group of scientists who had an apparent impact on other cultures which followed their creativity.

5- The emergence of an Islamic civilization characterized by comprehensiveness and profundity, thus making it at an acceptable level for other countries seeking to adopt them or a part of them as deemed fit and proper.

6- Facilitating the way for the scientists and scholars of both the medieval and modern age in completing what was provided by the Islamic civilization to the world, including scientific inventions, innovations and developments in all fields.

7- Widening the Arabic language with scientific terms and philosophical expressions derived through the translation of Islamic civilization into other languages.

8- Widening the scope of Arabic literature with the new expressions, ideas, meanings and characteristics inserted into it.

9- The trend of translation was the one paving the way for authoring, which benefited from translated heritage, and people were directed to science and to study for purely scientific motives.

10- Enriching the Islamic library; this had an impact, causing the emergence of numerous private, personal and public libraries.

11- The emergence of the idea of religious tolerance of free non-Muslims by making them closer to caliphs, princes and governors, and generously giving them consideration for the scientific efforts they exerted in translation.

12- Contributing to a keen interest in Islamic sciences and purifying them from external ideas after the emergence of what was called "the reaction" in the third of the translation stages in the Abbasid Era, especially when it was noted that there is an overlap with the beginning of the second stage.

According to the researcher, the most prominent negative results from the translation trend included the following:

1- Perhaps translation was the beginning of bad exploitation of religious tolerance by free non-Muslims. Translators did not consider this trait; they tried to intervene in criticizing some of the provisions of Sharia, such as the recommendation to drink wine and to keep listening to music, and this was also exploited in achieving political, ethnic or doctrinal ambitions.

2- Translation had an impact on fragmenting Islamic culture and supporting groups which opted to give priority to mind and reasoning, encouraged by caliphs who adopted their ideas. Such were ordeals like dark nights which true men encountered, to whom credit goes in preserving and protecting this religion. One of the prominent groups was Al-Mo'atazal, which had a high rank in the second of the translation stages in the Abbasid Era.

3- As a result of reliance upon the Syriac, a sentence came from Greek translations accompanied by obscene mistakes and works of falsified origin had jugglery and some rites inherited with philosophy; this caused confusion, and Muslims had to bear the burden of purification and rectification. A little bit leaked into Islamic thought, and confusion of translation continued through the other stages.

4- As a result of reliance upon non-specialized translators, translation was accompanied by a lack of accuracy and profundity, especially in identifying scientific terms and languages for translated subjects; this contributed to the above-mentioned confusion.

5- As a result of the reliance upon some Syriac translators, some translations were made which lacked scientific honesty; the Syriac had their impact in deleting some ideas which they regarded as being contradictory to their religious orientations. Most of them were Nastooris who vilified Jesus Christ (Peace of Allah be Upon Him); thus Syriac centres were established for the purpose of supporting their adopted ideas. This was reflected in their translation into Arabic or their translation from Syriac into Arabic.

6- There was a group of translators who did not master both the source and target languages perfectly. Some of them did not completely master either language. This had the effect of causing ideas to be unclear; the focus here is upon the lack of complete mastery qualifying a translator to translate from and into the language.

7- There was a group of translators who exploited the gluttony of caliphs, princes, governors and the wealthy and their fondness for science and generous giving to scientists; they used to translate a part of the book and make it an independent book and the other part as other independent books, and so on. The impact of this was to cause ideas in the original book not to be monotonous. They used to ascribe books wrongly to famous scientists for the purpose of receiving generous payment.

8- Translation was a wide field for orientalists in confirming their suspicions of Islamic sciences and their derivation from other previous sciences. In this, there is a confirmation of the non-originality of Islamic sciences, thus leading them to allege that Islam is all derived from previous cultures. This is because, as stated by orientalists, it is a grouping of Christian, Jewish, Greek and perhaps Indian and Persian cultures. This is noted when talking about the impact of translation and that it caused Muslims to know many sciences including Greek law, as they say, whose impacts were clear on the Islamic Fiqh and Arabic language.

9- In addition to blending with other cultures, translation contributed to confirm the concept of philosophy in Islam; thus, philosophy has become attributed to Islam as if it were one of the sciences of Muslims. Still today there is debate about the truth of this statement, as some debaters have moved from attributing this science to Islam to apparent denial against anyone opposing this ascription, and slandering them with negative attributes taken from other cultures.

10- Translation and contact with other countries contributed to confirming the concept of music, and, as a result of translating books in philosophy and music and the accompanying welcome they received from some caliphs, a level of listening and enjoyment was reached. Some believed that there is an Arab music or Islamic music and some rulers listening to music became a pretext that it was allowed to listen to music. (35)

If we take one example for the impact of translation – the cultural impact of translation – we will find the following:

1- Inside Arab Homeland:

On the basis of the contribution of translation, Arabs went ahead and their genius minds guided them to make discoveries and innovations in each and every art; they used to keep the sciences of others as a precedent to them and corrected whatever was in need of correction and also added considerably to what they discovered and experienced. They were not translators only as alleged by biased people; rather, they got into what we call the Arab Prosperity Age, which was an age for open-mindedness, scientific research and wide-scale authoring.

In mathematics, Arabs derived the numbering system from the Indians, adapted it and made it into two series: the first is known as Indian Numbers, which are now in use in the Arab East, and the zero in it is symbolized by a dot; the second series is known as Dusty Numbers, which were commonly used in Morocco, then moved to Europe; in these a zero is symbolized by a circle. To the Arabs is attributed the use of decimal statistics, the use of zero and the invention of decimal fractions, algebra, the solution of algebraic equations of the second degree and the use of symbols in algebra and trigonometry.

Great credit goes to the Arabs in astronomy due to their considerable contribution; most Arab scientists were in the field of mathematics; some of them invented astrolabe in a new form beneficial in the processes of observation, such as pinpointing heavenly bodies on the horizon, the calculation of time and the determination of distance from the equator. Some of them built observatories for their own astronomical research; others determined the radius of the Earth and of other planets.

In music, Arabs wrote many books and inferred many tunes as well as inventing musical instruments and developing existing ones.

The science of chemistry started very early in ancient nations such as Egypt, and the Greeks did not add anything to it. The first to work as a chemist was Khaled bin Yazeed (died in 85 Hijri), followed by Jaber bin Haiyan (died in 198 Hijri) who carried out pioneering research, experiments, additions in this science and he based it on experimentation. He was followed by Al-Kanadi, Al-Razi, Ibn Sina, Mohammad bin Abdul-Malek and Mansour Al-Kameli. (36)

In natural science, there were many scientists who corrected the mistakes of Iqlidis and Ptolemy and went through the experimental method; they established the modern science of light and created a pendulum seven centuries prior to Galileo. They set a schedule about qualitative weights of metals.

Arab scientists were very concerned with human biology, zoology and botany; however, this science was not always independent from other sciences, especially medicine, pharmacology and agriculture. It was often combined with them.

In medical sciences, Arab physicians assimilated the considerable amount of information translated from Greek and Indian; however, based on their scientific experiences, they later made corrections and additions to this information. Thus, they had their own discoveries and compilations which were translated into Latin and other European languages and thus it was the rationale and basis for progress in the modern era.

Agriculture was linked to medicine; Arabs developed agriculture, improved plants and studied different herbs, trees, seeds and fruits. The people of Al-Andalus were especially concerned with agriculture.

This intellectual renaissance, which was reached by the Arabs, came to fruition in every aspect of knowledge, something which cannot be discussed here in detail.

The scientific efforts of the Muslims aroused the admiration of fair Western historians and scientists; they bore witness to the achievements made by the Muslims. William Osler said, "If the Arabs are considered to have kindled their lamps from the Greek lamps, they have also become one glaring flame providing light to all the people of the Earth." Sarton said, "It is a great work that the Arabs translated the sciences and philosophy of the Greek and added to them to the extent that they caused such sciences and philosophy of the Greek to reach an honorable rank of development and growth." Sidio said, "Arabs were the professors of all Europe in all the branches of knowledge."

This renaissance widened its scope in space as it did in time; it was launched from Damascus and Baghdad, the capitals of the Umayyad and Abbasids caliphates. Then, it soon extended to the regions of the Arab Homeland and had a centre point in the east and west. Citizens of the Arab regions and Islamic countries took part in such a renaissance together, with the Arabic language acting as the organizer and cornerstone in it, giving free room for all types of knowledge into which the cultures were translated and in which the Arab scientists and scholars wrote down their books and compilations.

2- Outside Arab Homeland:

Over four centuries from the early 1100s AD (start of the Crusade Wars, 1096 - 1291) until the decline of Granada in 1492, the Arab Homeland was exposed to fierce invasions from the east and west. It had undergone ordeals and disasters as well as factors of weakness from the inside and outside thus causing disunion in place of union, separation instead of solidarity and weakness instead of power. An example of what happened was that the Tatars raided Bukhari Al-Zahira which contained population numbering more than 400,000 and left such a city as lifeless ruins. When they raided Baghdad, they killed about 800,000 persons and caused great destruction to occur. Ibn Khaldoun [37] says, "All the books during the conquest of Baghdad were thrown into the Tigris River. The Tatars made considerable destruction and burnt everything including books and libraries."

Thus, the time of prosperity of sciences and knowledge in the Arab world coincided with the time of the spread of ignorance in Europe, which was called the Medieval Ages. Jeboan says, [38] "The Arab age of science coincides with the darkest age of Europe and the one most full of ignorance; then the Arab age of science deteriorated afterwards."

With the start of Arab decline, the Europeans began to considerably derive from the Arab culture. They derived from Syria and Egypt during the crusade wars, and then from Sicily and South Italy in the era of Al-Aghalibah, and from Andalus in particular. They relied on translation in deriving the sciences from the Arabs; what they translated into their languages from Arabic constituted the basis for their modern scientific renaissance which started four centuries before and is still going on today.

It seems that the School of Medicine established in Salerno in South Italy was linked to the Arab Islamic culture in the tenth century (AD). Emperor Great Otto sent Jan Ghorts on a political mission to Andalus in 952 AD. He remained there for three years and returned with many Arabic books, thus causing interest in mathematics to appear in Lorin and Rine Basin in the eleventh century.

Perhaps the oldest translator of Arab scientific books into Latin was Constantine (died in 479 Hijri), who was born in Carthage and travelled to Islamic countries then became a monk in Casino Monastery in Italy in 1056 AD. In Toledo in Andalus, a school was established for translation from Arabic into Latin sponsored by its bishop Rimond (1125 – 1151). Translators in this school included Adellard, Roger and Mozli, who were English. Then the trend of translation moved to other cities such as Barcelona, Babylona and Shaqoobia in Spain, Bizaih, Narboona and Toloz in France.

One of the most famous translators was Gerard of Cremona, who was dispatched by Emperor Fredrick I who was concerned with astronomy from Crimona City where he lived in Toledo in Spain to obtain the book entitled *Almagest* by Ptolemy. No sooner had Gerard reached Toledo than he was so charmed by treasures of knowledge there that he stayed for twenty years, during which he translated not only *Almagest* but more than 80 manuscripts with which he returned to his homeland.

Among the books he gained on his journey were books of Hippocrates and Galenus, which were translated into Arabic by Hunain bin Isshaq, the book of Al-Mansouri by Al-Raazi, the book of surgery by Ibn Al-Qassem and the book of Law by Ibn Sina. Among them also was Jerbir Al-Oferoni, who was later promoted to Pope in 389 under the name of Selfestros II (died in 393 Hijri). He studied in Andalus at the hands of Arabs and translated numbers to Europe, and through this he facilitated the learning of arithmetic and astronomy. They also included Astafen Al-Antaki of Bizi origin (1194 – 1250 AD), Marcus Mikhael, Skoto Gerard de Sabionta, German Herman, English Alfred de Soishal who lived in the thirteenth century (AD) and French Jack Debarse (1380 – 1458 AD), etc. and others who translated scientific books into Latin.

Two of the great rulers of Europe in the thirteenth century were concerned with sponsoring the trend of translation, namely, Fredrick II (1215 – 1250 AD), Emperor of the Holy Roman Empire, King of Sicily and Germany, and Alfonso X, King of Kishtala, called the Wiseman (died in 1284 AD).

Thus, Europe could, over two centuries, derive knowledge from four cultures: Greek, Hellenic, Byzantine and Arab through translation, the bridge between cultures and nations.

The torrent overwhelmingly flows through the same; the following books were translated: in Badwa, *Kitab Al-Kolliyat* by Averroes (Ibn Roshd) and *Kitab Al-Taisir* (Book of Facilitation) by Ibn Zahr Al-Andalusi; in Sicily, *Kitab Al-Hawi* by Al-Razi. In addition, some books were translated more than once, such as *Kitab Al-Qanoon* (Book of Law) by Avicenna (Ibn Sina), Zaad Al-Mosaferin (Supplies of Travellers) by Ibn Al-Jazzar and other books by Al-Razi and Averroes.

Bint Al-Shati', Dr Aisha Abdul-Rahman, lists original heritage Arabic scientific books translated by Europeans in the preceding ages in order to learn from them; they were reprinted or retranslated in the modern age in appreciation of their value in the history of the development of science in the world.

The treatises of Jaber bin Haiyan (died in 198 Hijri) in chemistry were known by Europe in their Arabic texts and were translated into Latin and then German (Hollombard 1678 AD), then into English (Richard Russel 1928 AD).

Al-Khawrizmi's *Algebra and Opposition* (died in 236 Hijri) was translated into Latin by Gerard of Cremona, then Rozen published its Arabic text with an English text in 1850 AD.

Al-Razi's *Kitab Al-Hawi* (died in 311 Hijri) had been known in Europe since 1282 AD and was translated into Latin by Gerard of Cremona in 1486 AD. Al-Razi's *Treatise on Smallpox and Measles* was translated by Fala into Latin in 1498 AD, by Jubail into Greek in 1548 AD, by Paula into French in 1866 then by Leclaire and Lenoire in 1866 AD as well, and examples like this are numerous.

Sarton, in his book entitled *History of Sciences*, believed that it is better to divide his review about scientific achievements into ages, each of which spans a period of time being half a century and a century in each half of it there is one prominent century figure. He called the period from 400 to 450 BC the "Age of Plato", followed by the "Age of Aristotle", the "Age of Iqlidis" and the "Age of Archimedes", the period from 600 – 700 AD he dubbed the "Chinese Century". However, the period from 750 – 1100 AD (i.e. 350 continuous years), was a constant series of the ages of Jaber Ibn Haiyan, Al-Razi, Al-Masoudi, Abi Al-Wafaa, Al-Bairooni, Avicenna, Ibn Al-Haitham and Omar Al-Khaiyam, all of whom are affiliated to the Arab Islamic civilization.

The first European names appear after 1100 AD: Gerard of Cremona and Roger Beaco, and even the glories of this period over 250 years were shared by names such as Averroes (Ibn Roshd), Nasser Al-Din Al-Toosi and Ibn Al-Nafis.

After 1250 AD, the brilliance fades for a while, but soon non-stop brilliance resumed.

The Early European Renaissance came about after they had access to the Arab intellectual and scientific heritage; they started to feel deficient in comparison to the greatness of the Arab thought and its great impact; it was a mixture of astonishment, appreciation and admiration. Italian Poet Petrarch (1304 - 1374 AD) portrayed this condition when he addressed his nation indignantly saying, "What? If Cicero can become an orator after Demostinos and Virgil can become a poet after Homer, and then comes the Arab, no one is allowed to write? We kept up with the Greek and sometimes outdid them." They say, "We can not reach the rank reached by the Arabs." He says, "How insane! What a genius Italy is!"

Perhaps what the famous French thinker, Roger Garaudy, in his book entitled *Beyond Islam* (p. 140), said represents a summary of a prominent civilization event in the history of humanity which had, for its chronological and spatial expansion and vastness, a permanent impact, saying, "Arab Islamic civilization had enriched humanity throughout thousand of years and prepared them for the future. The Arab civilization translated across Sicily and Spain to Europe a culture whose suffering and aftermath was borne by the Arabs throughout ten centuries.

Through translation, these cultures began to revive. The contemporary West was born from the kings of Spain (Alfonso X) and Sicily (Fredrick II), both of whom were keen enthusiasts of Arab Islamic civilization – such Arab Islamic civilization which was the source for the West's civilization. (39).

1.5: The Importance and Results of Translation

This age witnesses an extraordinary revolution in human knowledge, whether in terms of quality or quantity. It especially witnesses successive and accelerating new developments in the field of science and technology. It is true to say that it is an age of knowledge explosion and scientific revolution.

Development accelerates where human potential and financial capabilities are available; however, on the contrary, development is slow-paced when such conditions are lacking or some are more available than others.

Thus, some countries in the world reached an advanced degree of development in the field of sciences and technology, while others, including our Arab countries, are still lagging behind or rather they are very slowly developing. With the passing of the years, the gap has widened between both parties, and the difference between them in the field of sciences and their application has become greater and greater.

First Requirement: The Importance of Translation:

People on this planet live in one age but in very different and disparate circumstances in standards of living and levels of income and economic and social growth. The gap becomes wider between those countries still creeping on the route of development and those having already achieved considerable progress in the same. Every day, a new discovery and invention is made while the other countries are still at the stage of receiving and in the state of consumption, have not yet arrived at the giving and production stage.

It is particularly noteworthy here to science and technology without overlooking the importance of literature and arts in forming man and building his culture for the purpose of directing attention towards the fact that having intellectual and technological potentials in this age is one of the most important prerequisites for enjoying supremacy and freedom, safeguarding national independence and protecting dignity. While lagging behind in science leads to retreat and falling victim to dependency in all fields.

One of the researchers says, "Arabs are now having a hard test and are at a crossroads; they can either keep gaspingly lagging behind the race, only consuming and not producing, dependent on an invasive culture, the captives of a developed world, buying their products and imitating them in their customs, traditions and taste, and even putting on their textiles and eating their canned food, or they can aspire to sources of knowledge without slowness to reach the limit reached by the developed and participate with them in creating what is new and innovating what is beneficial.

The first step on this way is to intensify and concentrate efforts on translating sciences into our Arabic language; the nations which preceded us in the civilization renaissance in this age went through this process.

The scientifically and technologically developed countries translate from one another's languages; therefore, we find that the trend of translation is flourishing among the English, French, German and Russian languages. There were many sincere calls, inviting a purposeful good translation trend to make us keep up with the scientific advancement.

One of the researchers wonders, "Is translation the only and sufficient prerequisite for creating a scientific renaissance in the Arab Homeland and consequently creating a general renaissance including all the aspects of life?"

He answers this question, saying, "Of course, it is not that simple; translation is not, at best, the only and sufficient prerequisite for creating a scientific renaissance in the Arab Homeland. However, there is no doubt that translation plays a major role in establishing Arab civilization in this age. It enables us to get rid of linguistic dependency and puts in our hands the means and tools of work, enabling us to stand at the threshold of this age full of everything new without abandoning our great heritage assimilated by our Arabic language and puts us in the state of readiness for action: positive action represented by participation in the human scientific effort in the world.

Then, there are some other matters; we can combine translation with what supports the building of Arab science and culture, by developing education in all its stages, especially the instruction of sciences at the university and postgraduate stages, by establishing centres for scientific research, restoring the immigrant minds whose intellectual and scientific potentials were lost by us, exploiting natural resources and manpower well, linking education to plans of social and economic development and by achieving Arab integration in all fields.

The researcher also believes that translation should be included within a comprehensive developmental plan within the educational, cultural, scientific and social strategies, in order that the trend of translation can take its natural place and produce favourable results.

We presently believe that translation is more active in the developed countries because of competition in the field of knowledge, especially scientific and technological knowledge, and keen interest in reviewing the discoveries of scientists and their research in other languages. This leads these countries to take care of translation. We find that the volume of what is translated from one of the languages is compatible or harmonious to scientifically, literarily or artistically innovative works achieved. (40)

Second Requirement: Results of Translation:
   When two cultures are blended, one of them should influence the other and vice versa, and this is normal. Due to their large-scale conquests, Arabs used to blend with many nations having different and even opposite ideologies; they influenced and were influenced by their ideas and theories. They practised such ideas on many occasions. Dr Taha Hussain says, All these cultures, whatever their capability to influence, met and gathered in the Islamic culture; they were digested and assimilated by the Arabs, got independent in the Abbasids Era and became considerably remote from their old origins where they can be said to be purely Islamic cultures.

   This all occurred through translation of all different types. Before we mention the impact of each of the most important civilizations separately, we would like to outline the results which arose from this good beneficial process, as referred to by one of the researchers, including the following:

1- The scope of Arab culture was widened through the cultures and thinking schools of other nations coming to it.
2- Arabs got access to sciences they were in need of, such as mathematics and medicine.
3- The Arabs were presented with an early opportunity to perform their mission in developing human culture.

The Arabs did not know foreign languages; if translators had not translated the sciences of India, Persia and Greece, they would not have been able to show their genius in such sciences, develop them and make them a source of prosperity for all humanity. If Arabs had waited to learn foreign languages and perform translation by themselves, at least a complete century would have passed before they would have been able to do this; Arabs might have lost, during that time, their love for science; their living conditions might have become unstable, or books of science remaining to their day might have been lost.

4- Arab civilization was developed and promoted in general scientific life in different sciences and arts.
5- Arabic language became full of scientific terminology and philosophical expressions.
6- Arab literature was developed in two aspects: through the arts, characteristics and meanings provided as a result of access to the

intellectual life of other nations on one hand; then by the natural leakage of a number of philosophical concepts and expressions or by derivation from the men of letters themselves.

7- Arabs made use of foreign measurements and concepts in handling several legal and linguistic sciences: in definition, division, logical methodology and proofs.

8- Emergence of Geniuses: It is known that when the age of translation was over and Arabs had gathered a tangible amount of books in each art, Muslims began to invent and make scientific productions in different fields of science, and unparalleled prominent figures appeared from among them as men of genius all over the world, which came as a result of such translation done by those translators.

9- Honesty in Accepting Religion: First of all, many people converted to Islam wishing to have money, position and protection. But when the Abbasid Era came and many books were translated and thought was developed in the Qur'an and Sunna through philosophy, logic and science, many people converted to Islam in admiration of the Qur'an and Suanna and in recognition of Islam's favour on other religions. (2)

1.6: Media Translation

Day after day, the features of the important role played by the mass media in guiding society and spreading awareness among its members become apparent. The mass media is needed to contribute to the process of development in all its fields, in addition to its role in meeting man's need for communication. It is a human need which developed with the evolution of human communities so that an individual can contact others and exchange information and ideas with them as well as express his or her inner feelings.

In the modern age, the media is no longer limited to satisfying interests and instilling information; rather, it has been transformed into creating interests and cultural reformulation in man through different arenas and developed technologies.

The mass media deal with many news items which come from several sources and are translated into all the languages of the world, and a great number of them are in need of being translated into the languages to be dealt with and in such a manner that meets the demands of the audience to which they are addressed.

Thus, media translation has become necessary and indispensable for all mass media and an urgent need imposed by requirements of professional work in each medium. Mastery of one foreign language, at least, is very important for those who want to get into media work and seek distinction in its field.

Colleges of media all over the world are keenly interested in introducing known international foreign languages in their courses, and in their graduates mastering as many languages as possible so that such graduates will keep up with the developments imposed by the nature of their work and with the professional characteristics required by the necessities of work in any mass media.

First Requirement: Mass Media and Newly Developing Languages:

Mass media means all the tools used in the industry of the media and conveying information to people; they are divided into visual, audio and audiovisual mass media. Visual mass media include books, newspapers, magazines and bulletins; audio media include radio and audio recorders; audiovisual media include television, video, cinema, internet and SMS sent by mobile phones.

These mass media deal in different languages and publish their news materials in several languages according to the audience they are addressing; these mass media include:

First: Newspapers and Magazines:

Newspapers have a high rank among all the mass media; in a number of areas they are considered to be the first mass media, followed up, admired and widespread. The glamour of newspapers has never faded, despite the advantages of other mass media like television and internet.

To keep up with scientific developments, press institutions not only issue paper newspapers to be distributed at certain times in the morning or evening; rather, they rely on the internet to issue electronic versions with continuous updates for their websites by publishing the most important developments and events that have occurred in all parts of the world; thus, they are still keeping cut-throat competition witnessed by such mass media.

Although newspapers have many peculiar advantages and characteristics, magazines can maintain a readership base and polarize a certain stratum which can not find their interest achieved in any other mass media.

Magazines seek to enhance their role through developing their various materials and keeping up with the technical age in terms of output touches, types and quality of paper, aesthetics of pictures, publishing an electronic version over the internet to increase and widen the scope of their readership with as large a circulation and as much accessibility as possible.

Second: Books and Reports:

Among the visual mass media, books and reports are considered as having special and limited influence and impact on a certain readership type in comparison to newspapers and magazines. This means that both means of information have an influence on a certain type of audience, which is the category following up books and reports and having enough special time for this as well as having a certain type of culture enabling them to comprehend the content of any book or report handling such issues.

Common to both these means of communication is the fact that they contain a considerable amount of information, detailed data, graphs, possibly profound research; thus, they give the reader an extensive understanding and comprehension for each issue. They are not used for current and immediate media coverage because they are not published on a daily or weekly basis.

Third: News Agencies:

News agencies play an important role in conveying and exchanging news; they impose themselves strongly upon different parts of the world and provide several services for subscribers and for people following up their news materials and different products. They contribute to making an impact on international public opinion and directing it into orientations suitable for their policies and the objectives of those undertaking and financing them.

Such news agencies developed over time, enhanced their role and spread to become the first means of information all over the world in terms of effect, efficiency, orientation and spread, with a slight noticeable reduction in the past decade because of the spread of satellite channels in most areas of the world and the increasing competition among them to win a stratum of as many people following up and subscribing as possible.

However, despite this cut-throat competition among satellite channels themselves on one hand and among satellite channels and news agencies on the other hand, the latter has continued to have greater influence and power and their share of the mass media market has ranged between 70 and 75 % as per the disparate statistics conducted by specialized national institutions from one period of time to another.

Over recent years, such news agencies have witnessed a remarkable development in their content, management and mechanisms of work; areas of spread, expansion and influence; use of the latest scientific and technological equipment; imports and external services and subscribers. This is in addition to the editing techniques used in them, the variety in using different news arts and developing them by introducing professional touches to them.

Fourth: Audio Mass Media:

Audio mass media are represented in one means: the radio, which is considered one of the easiest, most widespread and cheapest means of communication, able to reach the audience and penetrating the barriers of illiteracy and geography, as well as political restrictions.

Fifth: Audiovisual Mass Media:

Audiovisual mass media became the most powerful, attractive and influential means of information not only in most homes, but in a great number of buses and cars; they spread to each and every place after scientific development contributed to making them affordable, small in size and easy to use.

The main reason for this influence is the use of picture, animation, and colours, and their programmes are appropriate to all strata of society.

The most important of such means of information is television, which has several advantages like those of the radio, such as spread and usability, but it is distinct in that its programmes contain pictures, colours, animation, and enhancement of sound effects with clarifying talking pictures.

Sixth: Cinema:

Cinema is considered an effective means of addressing information to certain strata of society, using its optimal method in all professional and technical aspects. The cinema display combining technical picture, expressive sound and background music greatly influences the audience.

Seventh: Internet:

The world witnessed quantum leaps in the last three decades; every day, science began to come up with a new invention, wonderful achievement and exciting development. It has become necessary to keep up with every development in the world of science and knowledge, but at the same time it is impossible.

The most important means of information is the World Wide Web which has become basic in the countries of the developed world and a number of developing countries. It has also become familiar in the other countries of the world, especially for university students.

This World Wide Web has caused the whole world to become a small village where its members can easily and flexibly communicate with one another, receiving and taking as much science and knowledge as possible while sitting at their personal computers and having access to the current and past events of the world by sound or picture and exercising their right to give their opinions and comments on the issues posed for discussion and public opinion.

No Arab means of information can do without the process of media translation for several reasons, including the following:

1- A means of information can not fill its paper or spatial room by its own potentials only or by its own media material. Thus, it resorts to importing media materials from other mass media published in several languages.

2- No means of information can, by whatever material potentials, cover the whole world with a network of correspondents to furnish it with international and world news. Thus, they resort to dealing with the international and world mass media, translating the information, and publishing it in several world languages.

There is an important point to be mentioned in this regard, which is the influence of mass media ideology on translation; it is known that each means of information has its own orientations, policies, aims and objectives, depending on to the orientations, visions and opinions of those in charge.

This has a clear influence both on the quality and type of translated news materials and on how to dispose of them. Therefore, this in turn affects the performance and intentions of a translator and the degree of conformity between the effects and influences he aspires to for his translation and what is actually achieved at the level of the relationship with the other, i.e. viewer, listener or reader.

Second Requirement: Adaptation of Media Translation:

There is a thorny issue in the field of translation in general and in media translation in particular. This is related to the limits of adaptation in the translated material which the translator handles. This matter was extensively discussed in several books and studies, and those who are for or against adaptation in translation have their own points of view in this field.

Adaptation in translation stems from an urgent and pressing need to create communication after being liberated from close connection to some components of the source text and attempting to draft a new text that takes into full consideration the type of receiver and the new circumstances of receiving in the target language.

Pastan enumerates three elements causing a translator to use adaptation in the source text, the elements of which are as follows:

- Failure of literal translation when it has to do with playing with words or collocations.
- Differences between truth and reality expressed in the connotation of the target language.
- Conscious concern for changing the nature and type of source address, such as summarizing a text or simplifying a deeply specialized text to produce a new text which is comprehensible to the reader.

One of the researchers says that to this extent adaptation continues to be called translation because it does not seek adaptation in meaning by changing it or replacing it for a new meaning. However, whereas media translation seeks at most times to convey the news and share information with the readership, a target text should not cause the source text be kept away by changing it, removing anything or adding to its meaning. People working in the media field may resort at some times to a summary translation necessitated by the amount of space specified in a means of communication, which is acceptable if the meaning and main ideas are kept without extortion or deformation.

This adaptation does not mean addition to translation by introducing new ideas or paradoxes not mentioned in the source text for the purpose of an ideological use, attributing to the writer of the source text things that were not mentioned; rather, it could be used for creating communication with the receiving audience through a conscious change of the source text function (summarizing it, interpreting its ideas or simplifying its linguistic level…) without destroying the content of its ideas which form the general meaning.

This over-adaptation could lead to deviations and grave violations encroaching upon the essence of the meaning intended to be conveyed and deforming its content.

Third Requirement: Idiomatic Expressions:

The media translator encounters several problems in his work, requiring from him lots of effort, follow-up and reading to overcome them; such problems include idiomatic expressions used in a given language.

Linguistically speaking, *Istelah* (idiom) is the infinitive of *istalaha* (made an idiom or term); when a group of people are said to have *istalaha* (to have reconciled), the difference occurring between them has been removed. Thus, they *istalaha* on a given matter means they adopt it and agree upon it and the matter becomes adopted and agreed upon. Each language has its own idioms as each science has its own terms and idioms.

As Mr Ghossen says, English speakers use a great number of idiomatic expressions in their daily conversations and writings to the extent that many scholars describe this language as being an idiomatic language. Therefore, learners of English in different parts of the world find it very difficult to understand idiomatic structures.

In this regard, a translator shall endeavour as diligently as possible to know idiomatic expressions used in the language he is translating from and comprehend their meaning and significance so as to produce correct and clear translation.

Fourth Requirement: Essentials of Media Translation:

The process of translating a media type of text, of any style and source, goes through several steps taking the form of the integrated process, starting with selecting the material which will be translated and ending with editing it in a proper journalistic style and selecting a proper headline for it. Dr Mohammad Hosni Nasser outlines these steps as follows:

First: Selection of Publishable Media Text:

The selection of publishable and translatable media text relies on several foundations and criteria as follows:

1- Media Material:
    A- Conformity of the material with the editing policy and general orientations of the means of information.
    B- Available main news values in the foreign news material including timeliness, importance, benefit, psychological proximity, geographical proximity, volume, excitement, human interest and fame.

The editing policy of the means of information consists of a number of rules governing the selection of media material; the most important of these rules include the following:

- Nature of the medium's audience: Translatable news is selected according to the interests of the prospective readership, listeners or viewers whom the medium seeks to satisfy.
- Foreign policy of the state in which the medium works.

In addition to considering editing policy and foreign policy in selecting a media text for translation, it is necessary for the editor translator to stick to the professional rules governing the selection process. This means that the news values are available in the news material.

2- The Source Medium:
A- Availability of news material and completeness of its elements and angles.
B- Credibility of the source medium and its objectivity in handling events.
C- Medium being distinct in covering the news of the region from which the media material is taken, in addition to the specialization of the source in the translated material.

3- Personal Interests of Editor Translator:
This refers to an editor's preference to write and translate material about certain areas or countries, about certain political or economical events or in specialized media materials, in addition to his/her preferences for reading, listening and/or watching.

4- Time and Space:
This concerns the nature of the mass media work and whether, for example, it is a daily, weekly or monthly newspaper, or whether it is for a newspaper, magazine, radio or television. Thus, each type has its proper journalistic forms, external issues and news. It also refers to the time allowed for the editor to finish translation and editing and to the criterion of space in terms of the space allocated for publishing the translated topics in the means of information.

Second: Stages of Media Texts Translation & Editing:
This stage, which relies upon the practical experience of an editor in media translation and editing, involves the actual work of a translator editor. According to his experience, this stage is accomplished in one step, i.e. he translates and edits at the same time, or is divided into two stages, as follows:

1- Translating the media text from the source language to the target language of the medium.
2- Editing a translated text, putting it into a proper media style and ensuring that it is written according to the rules of press or radio media writing.

These two divisions are proper and apply to beginner editors in the departments of media translation, who start by being assigned to translate the text into Arabic, provided that another editor, having sufficient experience in media editing, shall carry out the editing process.

In the first stage, a translator should bear in mind a number of considerations related to the nature of the media text and its technical style, the method of translating media terms and expressions and the methods of manipulating the text so as to conform to the character and work nature of the medium.

Fifth Requirement: Television Translation:

Television translation is considered the most sublime art of media translation because it conveys sound and image, and therefore the translator should take into account the animation on the screen in addition to the words of the speakers, their facial expressions and gestures. Because of the considerable wide-scale spread of satellite channels, it has become necessary to translate what is displayed on such channels into languages known all over the world. It is no longer limited to movies and serials only; rather, there is translation for each and every type of material displayed on a satellite channel. There is a type of textual translation known as dubbing; a literal translation is made for what is being said, then certain technical processes are carried out so that it seems to the viewer that the people appearing on the screen are speaking in their own language and not in the source language of the programmes displayed.

Good dialogue in any television work gains the appreciation of all, but those who are attempting to make an in-depth study of it are few, according to the hierarchical order of relationships gaining interest in any work; it occupies the fourth rank, at its best, and then is followed by montage, filming and sound. By this, we do not mean that professors of the arts of cinema deliberately ignore dialogue and translation. Studying television works bears several complex and difficult issues. This necessitates one to be concerned about dialogue in these works, and consequently subtitles. Secondary material that is inserted within the making of these programmes becomes complicating.

However, conducting a survey or study about the potentials and limits of translation of subtitles in any television programmes, we will find a focus on a group of issues that are very far from studying the dialogue, the most important of which are related to standard behaviour (intellectual) for the subtitling. Hence, it can be said that the nature of subtitles and the restrictions imposed upon them occupy a great deal of interest; the need for translating and compressing speech into just two lines, and taking into consideration not wasting the information content, leads the translator to reduce the number of text words. It is also very important for a translator to be aware of the complexities of the text of television work; a type of synchronization should be established between the voice and the content of the subtitles and between the picture and the content of the subtitles. The translator is also encouraged to make use of the information provided to him by the picture.

However, on the other hand, television pictures may display certain shots, and the subtitle may be manipulated to conveying the balance between the words and the requirements of keeping those pictures. Therefore, what we call "Respect of Shots" could necessitate respect of balance with the rhythm of dialogue and the necessity of drafting the form and framework of the subtitle and distributing it over two lines.

In order for dialogue to achieve its goal in reaching scenes, its writer should rely on a certain number of the frequencies and characteristics of daily conversation and resort to facilitating words. These characteristics are necessarily reflected in the subtitles as well. The translator should mainly delete everything irrelevant from the translation so as to guarantee a proper understanding of the translation.

Then, what is regarded as important in the development of the television plot should be rephrased. Television dialogue is highly expressive and sound transmigration could entail some sort of extravagance and repetition. It is not necessary to translate everything as long as the translation guarantees that a message is delivered.

In general, those working in the media translation field should take into consideration three issues, as follows:

- A subtitle focuses on the need to make good simple sentences in terms of structure and organization and should be in one comprehensible unit (comprehensible sentence).
- The nature and type of television work will have characteristics which appear regularly in translation in such a system caring for how to talk in such manner suiting the type of work.
- Fictional television dialogue differs from regular daily conversation in some features and characteristics.

Sixth Requirement: Translation of Cinema Movies:

The translation of audiovisual works in all their forms, whether into the mother language or into a foreign language, plays a unique role in developing a national character and local styles. As one of the researchers says, "Conveyance of cultural values in translation displayed on the screen has gained only little interest in the fields of literature. This makes it one of the most pressing issues in the researches of translation studies."

All this means that there is a great influence for translation of movies; it is a goal that can be achieved through displaying the main techniques of movie translation and classifying it internationally and historically as well as the following analysis of translation in the dubbing, printed translation from the perspective of adding localization or foreignization to translation.

First of all, it can be said that each country develops its own traditions in translating movies and takes one of two main types of translation, i.e. dubbing or written translation, according to the interests of cinema. Sometimes, a third type of translation is adopted, i.e. adding a sound in a second language to the sound of dialogue or comment.

Translation of movies was relatively easy during the period of silent films, as subtitling used to interrupt the course of the film every few minutes. Therefore, it was possible to add translation in the required language easily and display it instead of the original subtitles.

Then, a problem occurred with the emergence of speech movies in the late 1920s. US companies tried to solve this problem by producing copies of the movie itself in several languages, using the same location and dialogue, but with other directors and actors.

It was soon discovered that this method was not profitable, especially since the movies were technically weak and did not attract audiences.

Studios, which were established in France, were adapted for the purpose of producing copies of the original movies, relying upon translation by dubbed voices.

In the age of telecommunications and multimedia, a world audience has developed, claiming the right to access all that is new, whether a movie, song or book. Therefore, demand has increased, for example, on the US production and as a reaction; this production has dumped the market.

In the contemporary cinema, translation is not made from one word into another word, but from one culture into another culture; a text is considered a part of the world, not a separated part of a language. Hence, a process of translation is considered as conveyance between two cultures, and this is what is determined by the value of the source culture and the target culture. English-speaking countries, especially the USA, have the upper hand, and they are the ones holding the strings in the cinema industry today.

Translation is always regarded with suspicion; it transforms foreign texts into national texts to merge them with the locally comprehensible linguistic and cultural values.

This process continues in all the stages of translation production, distribution and reception; it starts with selection of the text to be translated, which suits certain local values, and this process continues during the laying down of a translation strategy that rewrites the foreign text in local dialects.

Seventh Requirement: Problems of Media Translation & Solutions:

There is no doubt that the ability of translation to convey the media message or dialogue material in the dramatic programmes and movies relies upon the competence of the translator in the first place and his mastery of both languages, in the visual, audio or written field.

The more the similarity between both texts in terms of lexical items, sentences, content and verbal rhyme, the more enjoyment the viewer feels visually and intellectually; this means that the translator reflected the image as it is and did not portray an image of his own.

Basically, a viewer hopes to directly understand the work without a go-between. Consequently, being a go-between, rendering the linguistic content in the visual form, a translator should make the receiver, in this case the viewer, feel that the viewer's language deficiency is overcome by the translation which adds to enjoyment of viewing and the accomplishment of the translator. The competence of television translation relies on several elements, including the capacity of the screen, the duration of the written word's appearance for the speed of dialogue and the ability of the receiver to read and assimilate, i.e. the viewer's speed of reading which is on the average five seconds per sentence of at most eight words.

Therefore, a translator finds himself encountering a great challenge represented in the compromise between two languages and appropriation between two means of reading and understanding, each of which has its tools, concepts, culture and style in the construction of sentences.

Arabic is a fertile language and rich with concepts and meanings. The selection of words or equivalents needs a great deal of care and accuracy; for example, hawaa (air) can be hawaa, reeh, naseem, taiyar, sarsar, hoboob, and in English there are similar, even though less variables, like air, wind, breeze, gust, draft, etc.

These problems can be divided into two parts:

First: Linguistic Aspects:

The linguistic dilemma here lies in the quality of several media materials including everyday and specialized jargon, different dialects and accents.

Hence, the issue of specialization arises; an ordinary translator becomes specialized in a certain field such as engineering, medicine, etc. However, a media translator should not only be knowledgeable in all such specializations but also able to address the audience, according to their different cultural and cognitive levels, in language they can understand in relation to such different knowledge fields. In other words, a translator should simplify concepts, scientific and literary terms so that the average receiver can understand the intended message, whether this is, for example, in medicine, engineering, mathematics or literature, etc.

This normally places a heavy burden on the shoulders of a media translator; he should have full general knowledge in most fields and a linguistic repertoire that allows him to accurately and competently translate different aspects of knowledge for the viewer.

Problems of translation in television and cinema works also include, for example, non-clarity of voice, poor pronunciation and different dialects.

Second: Cultural Aspects:

Numerous cultures pervade the world of translation. The translation of Indian movies in particular is filled with cultural dimensions. Different aspects of life, customs and traditions, religious beliefs are manifested in translation. On many occasions, the translator finds that there is clear proximity between the cultures of nations; however, the difficulty arises when phrases or words relevant to religious concepts are used.

Hence, a translator should be careful when translating such phrases or words and should be also be cautious that they appear as used in their respective field.

Third: Factor of Time:

A translator working in the mass media is confronted with a particular problem related to the time allowed for him to accomplish the material he is translating. As the factor of time is very important for all means of information communication, it is necessary for a translator to accomplish the material assigned in a certain period of time. This imposes a great burden on the translator and puts him under considerable pressure, especially in that he is required to provide a text respecting the limitations of honesty and loyalty to the original and acceptance in the target language.

This matter sometimes causes a translator to fall into linguistic errors and expression faults; he might not produce translation in the required quality, in addition to making mistakes in translating a number of special terms in the material.

In this regard, a translator should be experienced in quickly accomplishing the assigned tasks and accustomed to the different styles encountered in the media field. He should harmonize idiomatic expressions, symbols and acronyms so that translation can be produced as free of mistakes as possible.

The issue of the length of time taken to accomplish media translation is related to several factors:

- The translator's enjoyment in handling a subject;
- Harmony with the topic;
- Difficulty or easiness of the topic;
- Translator's previous knowledge of the topic; and
- Method followed in translation.

Practical Applications

Section One
Translating pieces of news in different fields
Practical applications are regarded as the main factor for those who work in the field of media translation, as they enlighten them about the different styles adopted in this field. They also lead them to the different methods that translators use to tackle news articles; in this case, a translator is regarded as a translator and editor at the same time.

The following are some of these applications in the most important subjects covered by the mass media. I have tried to include examples in both Arabic and English, and gradually, one by one, these items become more difficult. I have also left some of the texts without translation to give an opportunity to those who are interested in undertaking the process of translation by themselves.

I have taken these texts from different sources (1), in addition to some of the newspapers, magazines and news agencies. I have summarized and manipulated some of these translations, to serve the nature of the book and the audience.

The most important references:

Full Reference in Translation (Arabic), International Language Centre, Cairo, Ed. 1, 2009.

Mistakes Committed by Translators (Arabic), Akram Moamen, Ibn Sina Publications, Cairo, Ed. 1, 2009.

Media Translation (Arabic), *Ibid*

Useful Materials in Translation (Arabic), *Ibid*.

Progress in Translation (Arabic), *Ibid*.

أولا – أخبار سياسية

First: Political News

(1

النص العربي:

Arabic Text:

استقبل حضرة صاحب السمو أمير البلاد الشيخ صباح الأحمد الجابر الصباح – حفظه الله ورعاه – في قصر السيف صباح اليوم صاحب السمو الملكي الأمير سعود بن عبدالرحمن بن ناصر بن عبدالعزيز آل سعود , وذلك بمناسبة زيارته للبلاد.

وقد حضر المقابلة نائب وزير شؤون الديوان الأميري الشيخ علي جراح الصباح , ورئيس جهاز متابعة الأداء الحكومي الشيخ محمد عبدالله المبارك الصباح.

النص الإنكليزي:

English Text:

His highness the Amir, Sheikh Sabah Al-Ahmad Al-Jaber Al-Sabah, this morning received at Seif Palace, His Royal Highness Price Saud Bin Abdul Rahman Bin Nasser Bin Abdul Azeez Al-Saud, currently visiting the country.

The meeting was attended by the Deputy Minister of the Amiri Diwan Affairs, Sheikh Ali Jarrah Al-Sabah and the Chief of the Apparatus in charge of Following-up the Government's Performance, Sheikh Mohammad Abdullah Al-Mubarak Al-Sabah.

(2

النص العربي:

Arabic Text:

استقبل حضرة صاحب السمو أمير البلاد الشيخ صباح الأحمد الجابر الصباح –حفظه الله
ورعاه – في قصر بيان صباح اليوم سمو ولي العهد الشيخ نواف الأحمد الجابر الصباح .

كما استقبل سموه – رعاه الله – في قصر بيان صباح اليوم معالي رئيس مجلس الأمة
جاسم محمد الخرافي .

واستقبل سموه – حفظه الله – في قصر بيان صباح اليوم سمو الشيخ ناصر المحمد الأحمد
الجابر الصباح رئيس مجلس الوزراء.

كما استقبل سموه – رعاه الله – في قصر بيان صباح اليوم معالي النائب الأول لرئيس
مجلس الوزراء ووزير الدفاع الشيخ جابر المبارك الحمد الصباح.

النص الإنكليزي

English Text:
His highness the Amir, Sheikh Sabah Al-Ahmad Al-Jaber Al-Sabah, this morning received at Bayan Palace, His Highness the Crown Prince, Sheikh Nawwaf Al-Ahmad Al-Jaber Al-Sabah.
- - -
His Highness the Amir then received the National Assembly Speaker, Jasem Mohammad Al-Khorafi.
His Highness the Amir also received His Highness Sheikh Nasser Al-Mohammad Al-Ahmad Al-Jaber Al-Sabah, the Prime Minister.
His Highness the Amir received the First Deputy Premier and Minister of Defense, Sheikh Jaber Al-Mubarak Al-Hamad Al-Sabah.

(3

النص العربي

Arabic Text:

اجتمع رئيس مجلس الأمة جاسم محمد الخرافي اليوم مع الممثل الخاص للأمين العام للأمم المتحدة في العراق ستيفان دي ميستورا والوفد المرافق له.

وأكد رئيس مجلس الأمة جاسم الخرافي خلال اللقاء حرص دولة الكويت على استمرار العلاقات الطيبة مع العراق , والعمل على حل القضايا العالقة بينهما في إطار القرارات الصادرة عن الأمم المتحدة وضمن القنوات والوسائل الرسمية منوها بأهمية دور الأمم المتحدة وجهودها في هذا الاتجاه.

وأعرب الخرافي عن أمله في أن يتوصل البلدان الشقيقان إلى حل جميع هذه القضايا بما يحفظ حقوق البلدين التي أقرتها الأمم المتحدة وبما يحفظ الاستقرار للمنطقة ويوحد الصف العربي.

من جهته أكد الممثل الخاص للأمين العام للأمم المتحدة في العراق السفير ستيفان دي ميستورا دعم الأمم المتحدة للعلاقات الوطيدة بين الكويت والعراق.

النص الإنكليزي:

English Text:

The National Assembly Speaker Jasem Mohammad Al Khorafi received at his office today, the special representative of the United Nations Secretary General in Baghdad, Stafan De Mistura, and his accompanying delegation.

Speaker Al Khorafi stressed In the meeting, Kuwait's keenness on maintaining good relations with the State of Iraq and sorting-out, all standing issues between the two countries in accordance with the U.N resolutions and through official channels.

The National Assembly speaker expressed hope that the two countries would work out solutions to these issues in a manner that preserves the rights of both countries which were sanctioned by the United Nations to maintain stability of the region, and preserve unity of Arab ranks.

Speaking at a press conference following the meeting, Ambassador De Mistura, voiced the UN's support for strong relations between Kuwait and Iraq.

(4

النص العربي:

Arabic Text:

أكد وزير الداخلية الفريق الركن المتقاعد الشيخ جابر خالد الصباح ضرورة تطبيق القوانين بحذافيرها معتبر أن سيادة القانون مبدأ أساسي في دولة المؤسسات وأن لا أحد فوق القانون.

وشدد وزير الداخلية على وجوب وضع الكويت أولا والحفاظ على أمنها واستقرارها ما يعني مواصلة اليقظة والجاهزية في ضوء المستجدات الأمنية في المنطقة.

النص الإنكليزي:

English Text:

The Minister of Interior, Sheikh Jaber Al Khaled Al Sabah stressed the need to literally implement lows.

The Minister of Interior added in a statement today that the rule of low was a basic principle in the State of Institutions and that nobody was above the low.

He emphasized that the preservation of the security and stability of the State of Kuwait was a priority and called on citizens to remain alert in the light of the security developments throughout the region.

(5

النص العربي:

Arabic Text:

أمريكا تحذر رعاياها في كوسوفو

حذرت وزارة الخارجية الأمريكية الرعايا الأمريكيين المقيمين في إقليم كوسوفو من احتمال تعرضهم للخطر داعية إياهم إلى توخي الحذر واتخاذ احتياطيات أمن مكثفة.

وقالت وزارة الخارجية الامريكية في تصريح صحفي الثلاثاء إن الولايات المتحدة حظرت على دبلوماسييها التنقل في القطاع الصربي من الإقليم دون موافقة السفير الأمريكي.

النص الإنكليزي:

English Text:

U.S Warns Americans in Kosovo

The United States has warned Americans in Kosovo to take extra safety precautions and banned its diplomats from traveling in the Serb sector without the U.S ambassador's approval, the US State Department said Tuesday.

6) النص العربي:

Arabic Text:

حكومة بورما تمنع اجتماعا للمعارضة

قالت مصادر المعارضة البورمية ومصادر صحفية في بورما اليوم الثلاثاء إن الحكومة العسكرية منعت اجتماعا سياسيا كان من المقرر أن تحضره زعيمة المعارضة ايونج سان سو كاي في مدينة مايانجون التي تبعد عن العاصمة البورمية رانجون نحو 11 كيلو مترا.

يُذكر أن "كاي" الفائزة بجائزة نوبل للسلام في عام 1991 كانت قد وضعت رهن الاعتقال في منزلها منذ أكثر من عامين.

ويعد الاجتماع الذي ألغته الحكومة هو الثاني الذي تشهده زعيمة المعارضة، بعد ان تم الإفراج عنها أخيرا.

النص الإنكليزي:

English Text:

Burma Government Blocks road, Stops Suu Kyi Meeting

Burma's military authorities Tuesday set up barricades and blocked opposition leader Aung san Suu Kyi from holding a political gathering in a small town outside the Capital, an opposition source and reporters said.

The gathering at Mayangon township, about 11 km from Rangoon, would have been the 1991 Nobel Peace winner's second political meeting outside the city since she was released from house arrest more than two years ago.

(7

النص العربي:

Arabic Text:

أزمة المصداقية

يواجه مجلس الأمن هذا الأسبوع تحدیًّا خطیرًا لمصداقيته والطريقة التي سيتعامل بها مع الأزمة العراقية ستحدد بشكل نهائي إذا ما كانت مسؤوليته هي الحفاظ على السلام العالمي من كونه مجرد منفذ لسياسات تصوغها وزارة الخارجية الأمريكية. كان من المقرر بالأمس أن يتلقى مجلس الأمن أدلة من وزير الخارجية الأمريكية "كولين باول" على صدق مزاعم واشنطن بأن بغداد قد خرقت قرار مجلس الأمن رقم 1441 .

لكن من منطلق البيانات التي صدرت عن واشنطن حتى الآن فمن الواضح أن باول عاد لواشنطن مسلحاً بالمؤشرات، أي بأدلة ظرفية وليست الأدلة الدامغة على صدق واشنطن. مثل هذه المؤشرات لسنا بحاجة إليها في هذا الوقت، بل نريد أدلة دامغة من النوع الذي أظهرته واشنطن أمام مجلس الأمن عام 1960 لإظهار أن كوبا تواطأت في إخفاء قذائف سوفيتية موجهة.

النص الإنكليزي:

English Text:
Crisis of credibility

This week the Security Council faces a serious challenge to its credibility. The way in which it deals with the Iraqi crisis will decide, once and for all, whether or not it has any continuing relevance when it comes to maintaining peace in the world or whether it will become little more than a backbench supporter of policies formulated by the US State Department. Yesterday the Security Council was scheduled to receive evidence from US Secretary of State Colin Powell in support of Washington's claims that Baghdad is in violation of UN resolution 1441. But judging by statements that have emerged from Washington so far it would appear that Colin Powell is going to Washington armed, at most, with indicators, i.e. circumstantial evidence rather than the hard proofs Washington insists it has in its possession. Such indicators are not what is needed at this time: rather, what is wanted is the kind of hard evidence Washington produced before the Security Council in 1960 to demonstrate Cuban complicity in the concealment of Soviet missiles.

(8

النص العربي:

Arabic Text:

افتتاح المؤتمر التاسع لوزراء خارجية التعاون الخليجي والتعاون الأوروبي

افتتح وزراء خارجية دول مجلس التعاون الخليجي ودول الاتحاد الأوروبي اجتماعهم المشترك التاسع في فندق شاطئ الجميرة بدبي.

وأكد راشد عبدالله النعيمي وزير خارجية دولة الإمارات العربية المتحدة في افتتاح الاجتماع أن أمن واستقرار منطقة الخليج واجب جماعي لكونه يهم جميع الأطراف مضيفا إن دول مجلس التعاون الخليجي تسعى بشدة للحفاظ على هذا الاستقرار من خلال جهودها الجادة لتسوية النزاعات.

وحث الوزير الإماراتي الدول التي تسعى إلى تطوير علاقاتها مع إيران على أن تأخذ في الاعتبار أن تقوية ودعم الأمن والاستقرار في منطقة الخليج يتطلب تسوية النزاع حول جزر الإمارات الثلاث طنب الكبرى وطنب الصغرى وأبو موسى.

وأعرب النعيمي عن تقدير الدول الأعضاء في مجلس التعاون الخليجي الشديد للدور المهم والإيجابي الذي تلعبه دول الاتحاد الأوروبي في المساعدة على حفظ الأمن والاستقرار في منطقة الخليج.

وجدد دعوة بلاده إلى تسوية النزاع حول الجزر مع إيران التي اتهمها بالفشل في تقديم رد إيجابي على دعوة الإمارات المتكررة لحل النزاع من خلال المحادثات الثنائية أو من خلال التحكيم الدولي.

ودعا وزير الخارجية الإماراتي في الوقت نفسه إلى وضع حد سريع للمعاناة والظروف القاسية التي يعيشها الشعب العراقي وحث العراق على احترام قرارات الأمم المتحدة بما فيها إعادة الأسرى الكويتيين وإعادة الممتلكات المنهوبة إلى الكويت.

النص الإنكليزي:

English Text:

GCC, EU Foreign Ministers open discussion

The foreign ministers of the GCC and EU countries opened their 9th joint meeting at the Dubai-based Jumira Beach Hotel. Opening the meeting, UAE foreign minister Rashid Abdullah al Nueimi stressed security and stability in the gulf region were a collective duty as it was in the interest of all sides, noting the GCC countries were very keen to maintain such stability through serious efforts to settle standing disputes.

The minister urged countries seeking to develop their relations with Iran to take into account the need for consolidating security and stability in the Gulf, for an eventual settlement of a dispute over UAE greater and lesser Tunbs and Abu Mousa Islands. The GCC member state highly appreciated the important and positive role being played by the EU countries in helping safeguard security and stability in the Gulf, al Nueimi said.

He reiterated his country's calls for a settlement of the island dispute with Iran which he accused of failing so far to respond positively to a repeated UAE proposal to resolve the dispute through bilateral talks or by International Court ruling.

Meantime the UAE foreign minister called for a quick end to the suffering and severe circumstances being endured by the Iraqi people, urging Iraq at the same time to honor the relevant UN resolutions including the repatriation of the Kuwaiti prisoners and looted property.

(9

القوات الجزائرية تقتل 8 مسلحين ومصرع أربعة أطفال في انفجار قنبلة

لقي ثمانية من الإسلاميين المسلحين مصرعهم على أيدي القوات الحكومية فيما قتل أربعة تلاميذ عقب إصابتهم في انفجار قنبلة نهاية الأسبوع الماضي.

وقالت صحيفة لوكودتيان دي لوران الجزائرية إن المسلحين قتلوا في معركة مع القوات الحكومية في قرية سيدي بوبكر جنوب غرب محافظة صيدا.

وكانت الصحف المحلية قد أشارت إلى مصرع نحو 400 من المسلحين في نفس المحافظة وذلك في هجوم كبير شنته القوات الحكومية في مطلع الشهر الحالي.

وأكدت صحيفة لوكودتيان مصرع أربعة من تلاميذ المدارس يوم الاثنين الماضي نتيجة انفجار قنبلة يوم الأحد بالقرب من مدرستهم في مدينة خميس الواقعة على بعد 100 كيلو متر جنوب غرب الجزائر العاصمة فيما أصيب 24 آخرون في نفس الانفجار.

من ناحية أخرى قالت صحيفة ليبرتي الجزائرية اليومية إن شخصا واحدا قتل يوم الاثنين الماضي في انفجار قنبلة زرعها أحد المسلحين في حقل قمح في منطقة لخضرية الواقعة على بعد 70 كيلو مترا شرق العاصمة.

يذكر أن أكثر من 65 ألف شخص لقوا مصرعهم في الجزائر في أحداث العنف التي اندلعت في البلاد بداية عام 1992 وذلك على أثر إلغاء السلطات الانتخابات العامة التي حقق فيها الإسلاميون تقدما ملحوظا.

النص الإنكليزي:

English Text:

Algeria troops kill rebels, 4 boys die
of bomb wounds

Algerian troops shot dead eight Moslem rebels and four schoolboys died after succumbing to wounds from a weekend bombing local newspapers said on Tuesday.

The rebels were killed on Sunday in clash with government troops in sidi Boubekeur village in the southwestern province of Saida, Le Quotidien d'Oran said.

Earlier this month, local dailies said troops were encircling up to 400 rebels in the province in a huge military offensive.

Le Quotidien also reported four boys died on Monday from wounds they suffered when a bomb exploded on Sunday near their school in Khemis town, 110 km (60 miles) southwest of Algiers.

The authorities had said four people were killed and 24 wounded in the blast, the latest in a series of bombings in which thousands of civilians have been killed in the past six years.

Liberte daily said a bomb, planted by suspected rebels in a wheat field in the Lkhdaria area, 70 km (40 miles) east of Algiers, killed one person on Monday.

Algeria has been tormented by violence since early 1992 when the authorities cancelled a general election in which radical Islamists had taken a commanding lead.

More than 65,000 people have been killed since then, according to Western estimates.

(10
النص العربي

Arabic Text:

سمو امير البلاد يفتتح الخميس المقبل مدرسة إسلامية بمدينة نيويورك

يفتتح سمو أمير البلاد الشيخ صباح الأحمد الجابر الصباح يوم الخميس الموافـق 30 يوليـو مدرسة إسلامية تابعة للمركز الثقافي الإسلامي بمدينة نيويـورك لـدعم الخـدمات التعليميـة والاجتماعية التي يقدمها المركز إلى الجالية الإسلامية في المدينة.

وقال المندوب الدائم لدولة الكويت لدى الامم المتحدة ورئيس مجلس أمناء المركـز الـسفير عبد الله أحمد المراد في مقابلة مع وكالة الانباء الكويتية (كونا) "إننا نتشرف بأن يقوم صـاحب السمو أمير البلاد الشيخ صباح الأحمد الجابر الصباح حفظه الله ورعاه بنفـسه بافتتـاح هـذه المدرسة التي ستكون منبرللإنارة بكل ما هو متعلق في ديننا الحنيف".

واضاف إنه ستكون للمدرسة أهمية كبيرة لدى الجالية الإسلامية في نيويورك لأنهــا ســتقدم لأبنائهم وبناتهم تعليم الدين الإسلامي الحنيف واللغة العربية.

وذكر أن افتتاح هذه المدرسة من طرف صاحب السمو يعكس اهتمــام ســموه لــيس فقــط بالمدرسة وإنما أيضا بالمركز الإسلامي ككل ، فقد كان لسموه منذ أن كان وزيــرا للخارجيــة ومنذ بداية إنشاء المسجد الخاص بالمركز اهتمام خاص بأنشطة المركز التي منحها باستمرار رعاية خاصة ودعمها معنويا وماديا.

وبين أن المدرسة التي تمثل تحقيق حلم طال انتظاره ستبدأ أعمالها في بداية السنة الدراسية المقبلة في سبتمبر ، وستكون مدرسة نظامية وفق نظام التعليم الأمريكي وسيمون معترفـا بهــا من قبل وزارة التعليم مضيفا إنه يوجد حاليا نحو 200 طفل يتابعون الدروس الدينيــة ودروس اللغة العربية في العطل الأسبوعية والدورية.

وقال إن تمويل المدرسة سيكون من خلال المركز الإسلامي الذي تصله تبرعات من الــدول الإسلامية والأفراد ومن الرسوم التي يقدمها أسر التلاميذ ومن الدخل السنوي للمجمع الــسكني المبني فوق أرض المركز.

وذكر أن للمركز أنشطة دينية وثقافية وتوعوية موجهة إلى الجالية الإسلامية وبخاصة إلــى الأمريكيين الذين اعتنقوا الدين الإسلامي والذي يتزايد عددهم يوما بعد يوم.

وأعرب السفير المراد عن أمله في أن يزداد عدد المساجد وأن تتعزز ميزانياتها ويزداد مـــا تتلقاه من تبرعات لتمويل احتياجات الجالية الإسلامية التي تزايد عددها إلى درجة أصبح معهـا المسجدان الحاليان لا يفيان بالحاجة.

وأقيمت المدرسة التي تقدم تعليما حتى الصف السادس في الطابقين الأول والثاني من مبنــى مجاور للمركز وعلى أرضه وهي تحتوي على 13 غرفة تدريس وغرفة مخصصة لاجتماعات هيئة المدرسين وقاعة مؤتمرات تتسع لـ500 شخص وقاعة للتمارين الرياضية ومكتبة وجهزت المدرسة بوسائل التعليم العصرية واتسم تصميمها بأشكال وألوان ساطعة زاهية تشجع الأطفال على الدراسة.

وكانت دولة الكويت قد تبرعت بثلثي ميزانية بناء المركز الإسلامي الــذي بلغــت تكــاليف إنشائه نحو 17 مليون دولار ودشنه سنة 1991 المغفور له الأمير الراحل الشيخ جابر الأحمــد الصباح الذي كان له دور بارز جدا في إنشاء المسجد حيث تبرع بـ5ر1 مليون دولار شخصيا لبناء منارته.

والمركز لايخدم المسلمين فقط في مجال أداء شعائرهم الدينية بل يعـــرف أيـــضا مختلــف الجاليات الاخرى بجميع جوانب الإسلام ويساهم في نشر رسالة الإسلام والثقافة الإسلامية فـــي هذا الجزء من العالم.

والكويت وماليزيا والمغرب في طليعة الدول الإسلامية التي تساهم بتقديم التبرعات لتمويــل احتياجات المركز على أساس سنوي مستمر وتبلغ نفقات المركز نحو 700 الف دولار سنويا.

ومنذ 11 سبتمبر 2001 شرع المركز الذي تتسع قاعة الصلاة فيه إلى نحو 800 شخص في تنظيم منتدى خاص يدعى (المحفل الإسلامي لغير المسلمين) للتعريف بالإســـلام والـــرد علـــى الأسئلة والاستفسارات حول الإسلام والمسلمين.

وزار المركز العديد من كبار موظفي المدينة من بينهم عمدة المدينة مايكل بلومبيرغ.

ويقدم المركز منذ تأسيسه خدمات جليلة إلى الجالية الإسلامية في مدينة نيويورك وضواحيها ونجح في تقديم صورة إيجابية عن الإسلام والمسلمين للمجتمع الأمريكي وســـاهم فـــي إقامـــة جسور التفاهم بين المسلمين وغيرهم من سكان المدينة.

وقال مدير مشروع بناء المدرسة رالف أوتايانو ل"كونا" إن هذا المشروع "يعزز العمل القيم الذي يقوم به المركز في خدمة الجالية الإسلامية ونحن فخورون بإسهامنا في مساعدة هذه الفئة القيمة من سكان المدينة على بلوغ أهدافها.

النص الإنكليزي:

English Text:

Kuwaiti Amir to inaugurate Islamic school in NY on Thursday

His Highness the Amir of Kuwait Sheikh Sabah Al-Ahmad Al-Jaber Al-Sabah will inaugurate on Thursday the Islamic Cultural Center of New York's Islamic School, aimed at supporting the educational and social services that the center provides to the Muslim community in the city.

"It is an honor for us that His Highness the Amir Sheikh Sabah Al-Ahmad Al-Jaber Al-Sabah is personally inaugurating this school, which will be a shining beacon for all that is related to our religion (Islam)", said Kuwait's Permanent Representative to the UN and Chairman of the Center's Board of Trustees, Ambassador Abdullah Al-Murad, in a statement to KUNA on Tuesday.

The school will be of great importance to the Muslim community in New York, as it will help children and young people learn more about their religion and the Arabic language, he said.

Al-Murad noted that His Highness the Amir's inauguration of this school reflected his interest in supporting the center as a whole, noting that back at the time when he was foreign minister, His Highness Sheikh Sabah paid special attention to the construction of the center's mosque and its activities, and provided his moral and financial support to the project.

This school is the long-awaited dream of many, he said, adding that students would be enrolled as of September and that classes would be accredited by the US authorities as it would follow the acknowledged educational system here.

Some 200 children are currently taking courses and weekly classes in religious and Arabic studies, he added, noting that funding would be through the center, which collected contributions from Muslim countries and individuals, as well as annual tuition fees and income from the residential complex built for the center.

Al-Murad highlighted the religious, cultural and awareness activities of the center, directed at the Muslim community, especially converted Americans whose numbers were increasing day by day.

He hoped that more mosques would be constructed in the city, as the standing two no longer accommodated the needs of the growing community.

The school, which will provide schooling up to the sixth grade, is a two-storey building standing next to the center. It comprises 13 class rooms, a staff meeting room, a 500-seat conference hall, a gym, and a library. It is equipped with all necessary requirements, and is painted in bright colors that are most attractive to children.

Kuwait had donated two thirds of USD 17 million required to build the center, which was inaugurated in 1991, and the late Amir Sheikh Jaber Al-Ahmad Al-Jaber Al-Sabah donated USD 1.5 million to construct the mosque's minaret.

The center not only accommodates Muslims in their performance of religious practices, but also introduces other communities to the religion of Islam and spreads the word about Muslim culture in this part of the world. Kuwait, Malaysia and Morocco are among the leading contributors to the annual budget of the center, which comes to around USD 700,000.

Since the September 11, 2001 attacks, the center has been holding a forum for non-Muslims, aimed at responding to their inquiries about the religion. Since its establishment, the center - which has been visited by top New York officials, including Mayor Michael Bloomberg - has succeeded in highlighting the positive image of Islam.

Meanwhile, the school project manager, Ralph Ottaiano, told KUNA that the project would boost the valuable services the center provided to the Muslim community, and expressed pride in having contributed to efforts to assist this valuable segment of the society in its strive to achieve its goals.

(11

النص العربي:

Arabic Text:

انقسامات داخل وكالة المخابرات المركزية الأمريكية

تركز العديد من التقارير التى كتبت عن الانقسامات الحادثة داخل وكالة المخابرات المركزية الأمريكية على مديرها الجديد بورتر جويس الذي وصل إلى رئاسة الوكالة وكان عضواً بالكونغرس عن الحزب الجمهوري، وهو الذى أعلن عن توليه المنصب قبيل الانتخابات الرئاسية بقليل ويحمل خطة عمل واضحة .

فهو يرى أنه لا مناص من التغيير بعد مسلسل الفشل الذي منيت به بالوكالة، والذى كانت آخر صوره ادعاء امتلاك العراق لأسلحة دمار شامل .

لكن خططه واجهت رفضاً من مسؤولي الوكالة البارزين والقدامى ، وترك بعضهم الوكالة فعلاً والبعض الآخر هدد بالاستقالة .

وليس هناك شك في أن جويس رجل له آراء قوية وحين التقيت به قبل أن يعين مديراً لوكالة المخابرات المركزية قال لي بوضوح إن الوكالة فشلت في أداء مهمتها الأساسية .

وأضاف "إن المهمة الأساسية للمخابرات هي التجسس ، وهذا يعنى الوصول إلى أهداف صعبة ، تتطلب مخاطرة كبيرة".

ويرى جويس أن الوكالة تحتاج إلى تجنيد ضباط متخفين يعرفون كيف يستخدمون العملاء ويوجهونهم إلى الأهداف الصعبة ، ويستخدمون كل المهارات التي تتطلبها المهنة .

ويقول " هذه هي الأشياء التي فرطنا فيها ، وفجأة وجدنا أنفسنا لا نتوقف فقط عن الاستثمار ، بل نسرف في التفريط في مهمتنا الأساسية خلال حقبة التسعينات .

وحذر جويس قائلاً إننا لا نحتاج الآن لمجرد زيادة في الاستثمار بل نحتاج إلى طفرة حقيقية فعلاً في جهاز الخدمة السرية الذي يجند الجواسيس في قطاعات المخابرات .

وأوضح أن هذا التغيير لا يعني المناصب والأشخاص فقط ولكن يعني كل مؤسسات المخابرات . ويؤكد مؤيدو جويس أن التوتر الحالى ينبع من البيروقراطية المتأصلة في الجهاز والتي ترفض تحسين أدائها .

ويشير المراقبون إلى أن جويس يعتمد على مجموعة صغيرة من المساعدين جاء بهم معه من الكونغرس وهم غير قادرين على أن يتأقلموا مع الآخرين .

النص الإنكليزي:
English Text:
Dissentions in the CIA

The reports on the dissentions in the CIA is centered around the new CIA director Porter Joyce who holds now the position of the CIA director, and who was an ex-member of the Republican Party in the American congress. He divulged the fact that he has become the new CIA director just before the presidential elections, and that he has a clear work-plan.

In his opinion, change is inevitable after a series of failures from the CIA, especially the last episode of claiming that Iraq owns WMDs (Weapons of Mass Destruction).

But his plans were met with resistance from leading and veteran people in the CIA, and some tendered their resignation, whereas others threatened to quit.

No doubt, that Joyce is a man of strong will and determination, and when I have met him before he was assigned as CIA director he said clearly that the CIA has failed in performing its main mission.

He said to me, "The main mission of the Central Intelligence is spying, which means reaching difficult goals and higher risks".

In his opinion, the CIA needs to employ secret police officers who know how to deal with agents and how to direct them to difficult goals, and who use all the skills needed in such kind of a profession.

These are things that we have done without, then we found ourselves unable to stop investing, and we exaggerated in leaving our main mission during 1990s. Joyce warned that we do not need an increase in investment, but a real, big leap into the secret service that recruit spies in all CIA sectors.

Joyce said that this change does not mean only positions and men, but it means to change all the institutions of the CIA apparatus. Supporters of Joyce argue that the present tension is due to the resistance of deep-rooted bureaucracy that defies change that means to improve its performance.

Supervisors said that Joyce depends on a small group of assistants whom he brought from the Congress, and these people are unable to make themselves, acceptable to others.

(12

النص العربي:

Arabic Text:

الحوار مع حماس خطوة نحو السلام

إن أول رد فعل على كلام باراك أوباما بأنه مستعد للاتصال مع حماس – و لو على مستوى منخفض و بسرية تامة– يجب أن يكون حذرا .

وقد يعود ذلك الى أن الكشف عن مثل هذا التحرك يمكن أن يجعل احتمال حدوثه قليلا. فإذا ما وقع معسكر أوباما تحت ضغط انتقادات كبيرة من أولئك المعارضين لأي اتصال مع حماس فإنه قد يضطر الى إنكار هذه الفكرة و التخلي عنها. لقد كان أوباما حذرا من قول أي شيء خلال أزمة غزة, و بالطبع فهو لم يقم بأي عمل يناقض إدارة بوش. و بالطبع لم يختر أن يحدث أي تغيير سياسي علني. (و لكن بالطبع فقد تم الترحيب به في العالم الإسلامي الذي أغضبه صمته المفترض خلال الأسابيع السابقة).

أما الأمر الآخر فهو أنه حتى الانفتاح المحدود الموضوع تحت النقاش في الدوائر القريبة من أوباما هو أمر مشروط. فهو يبدو قائما إما على تلقي حماس ضربة قوية في غزة أو على المصالحة مع حركة فتح. و ليس هناك أي من هذين الأمرين مضمون الحصول .

و بالرغم من ذلك, فإن أولئك الذين اعتقدوا لفترة طويلة بأن السلام يعتمد على إدخال جميع الأطراف المشتركة في النزاع في الحوار و بأن السلام يصنع مع الأعداء و ليس مع الأصدقاء لديهم سبب ليحتفلوا بهذه الأخبار الجديدة, على الرغم من أنها تجريبية حتى الآن .

إن هذا الأمر يوحي بأن أوباما يريد أن يتابع المبادئ التي رددها مرارا و تكرارا في حملته الانتخابية عام 2008 ، و هي أن الدبلوماسية ليست نوعا من الجوائز للتصرفات الجيدة, و لكنها مكون مهم تمتلكه الدولة. إن الولايات المتحدة لن تطرح استخدام القوة لدعم مصالحها الحيوية, ومع ذلك فإن إدارة بوش أنكرت أن الدبلوماسية أداة مهمة عندما تعلق الأمر بالظلام الخارجي: محور الشر المكون من العراق و إيران و كوريا الشمالية إضافة الى سوريا و بالطبع حماس .

النص الإنكليزي:

English Text:

Talking to Hamas is a step toward peace

The first response to word that Barack Obama is prepared to make contact – albeit low-level and clandestine – with Hamas should be caution.

For one thing, the very act of revealing such a move can make it less likely. If the Obama camp comes under heavy criticism from those opposed to engagement with Hamas, it may be forced to deny it countenanced the idea at all. Obama has been super-careful to say next to nothing during the Gaza crisis – and certainly nothing at odds with the Bush administration. He would clearly not have chosen to make this policy shift public. (That said, it's bound to be welcomed by those in the Muslim world who have been angered by his virtual silence this last fortnight.)

Second, even the limited opening to Hamas apparently under discussion in the Obama circle is pretty conditional. It seems to be premised either on Hamas taking a "decisive drubbing" in Gaza or on a reconciliation with Fatah. Neither of those outcomes is guaranteed.

Nevertheless, those of us who have long believed that peace depends on engaging with all parties to a conflict – and that peace is made with your enemies rather than with your friends – have reason to be cheered by this news, tentative as it is.

It suggests that Obama means to follow through on the principle he articulated repeatedly in the 2008 election campaign: that diplomacy is not some kind of reward for good behaviour, but rather an essential component in any nation's toolkit. The US would never foreswear the use of force to advance its vital interests, yet the Bush administration did precisely that with diplomacy – denying itself that essential tool when it came to the nations it consigned to outer darkness: the axis of evil trio of Iraq, Iran and North Korea, along with Syria and, of course, Hamas.

(13

النص العربي:

Arabic Text:

تحييد الحلّ الفلسطيني عن الخلاف النووي مع إيران

أهم امتحان يخوضه الرئيس الأمريكي باراك أوباما في سعيه وراء صنع السلام في منطقة الشرق الأوسط لن يكون امتحان النيات والعزم والإيمان بالقدرة على تحقيق هدف حل الدولتين, قيام دولة فلسطين بجانب اسرائيل آمنة.

إن الامتحان سيكمن في الخطوات التي سيتخذها الرئيس الأمريكي سعياً وراء سلام عربي – إسرائيلي وما إذا كانت ستخضع لمجرد ما هو عملي و «في المستطاع» بدلاً من التمسك

بالاطر الأساسية الواضحة لذلك السلام والتي تتمتع بإجماع دولي ولها ما يكفي من مرجعيات وشرعية.

فإذا أخفق في تأكيد ما يجب القيام به وسمح بالاكتفاء بما هو في الامكان, يغامر الرئيس الأمريكي بتقويض المبادئ الضرورية للحل والسلام العادل ويعرض العملية التفاوضية نفسها الى تهديد خطير ومكلف لكامل المنطقة.

إدارة أوباما محقة في انتظارها استكمال زيارات مهمة لقيادات فلسطين وإسرائيل ومصر الشهر المقبل قبل أن تتقدم بتصورها المتكامل للخطوات الضرورية نحو السلام. إنما الاختبار الحقيقي لها سيأتي قبل التوصل إلى الحصيلة الأخيرة والخطة المتكاملة وسيكمن في كيفية تعاملها مع معادلة ما هو ضروري وما هو في المستطاع.

فالإطار التفاوضي ليس متوازناً وأدوات المساومة غزيرة في أيدي اسرائيل وشحيحة في أيدي الفلسطينيين. الأمر الذي يجعل التلاعب بــ «المستطاع» سياسة إسرائيلية مفيدة لحكومة لا تريد حل الدولتين ولا تريد دولة فلسطينية كحكومة بنيامين نتانياهو الذي أقحم إيران على فلسطين في بدعة هدفها الانقلاب التعجيزي على الرئيس الأمريكي والتزامه بقيام الدولة الفلسطينية.

فإيقاف ايران عن سعيها وراء السلاح النووي وتقييد نفوذها الاقليمي الصاعد هو موقف يحق لرئيس الوزراء الاسرائيلي أن يطرحه ويصرّ عليه إذا شاء. أما أن يجعل هذا الهدف شرطاً مسبقاً لانخراطه في مفاوضات سلمية حقيقية لمعالجة النزاع الفلسطيني – الاسرائيلي, فإن ذلك يستدعي مواقف أمريكية وروسية وأوروبية وصينية على سكتين متوازيتين انما هما منفصلتان: كبح ايران عن طموحاتها النووية وعن الهيمنة الاقليمية, والضغط على اسرائيل بحدية لتكف عن المناورة في عملية السلام.

العاهل الأردني الملك عبدالله الثاني حمل هذا الاسبوع الى الرئيس الأمريكي رسالة عربية فحواها أن حل الصراع الفلسطيني – الاسرائيلي هو المدخل الى حل شتى قضايا المنطقة, أي إن فلسطين هي المدخل لمعالجة المسائل العالقة مع ايران. فطهران تستخدم المسألة الفلسطينية لحشد الدعم وراء طموحاتها بهيمنة اقليمية وهي التي توفر الدعم العملي لــ «حماس» في فلسطين و «حزب الله» في لبنان رفضاً لحل سلمي قائم على المفاوضات ورفضاً لمبادرة السلام العربية القائمة على القبول بإسرائيل والتطبيع معها مقابل انسحابها الى حدود هزيمة 1967 وإنشاء الدولة الفلسطينية مكان الاحتلال.

فإذا بقيت مسألة فلسطين من دون حل, فالمستفيد هم الملالي والثورجيون في طهران وكذلك
قوى التطرف ومعها قوى الغضب المتصاعدة التي قد تهجر أحلامها بالسلام بسبب وضوح
التملص الاسرائيلي الدائم من الحل السلمي.

باراك أوباما مقتنع بأن فلسطين مفتاح رئيسي لمعالجة مختلف قضايا المنطقة ولن يوافق رأي
نتانياهو الرامي الى تجميد محادثات السلام في شأن فلسطين الى حين وضوح نجاح الجهود
الأمريكية مع ايران لوقف طموحاتها النووية والاقليمية. فهذه مواقف زائفة يمكن أن تجعل من
البدعة مزحة لو لم يكن الموضوع بهذه الجدية.

النص الإنكليزي:

English Text:
Keeping the Palestinian Solution Separate from the
Nuclear Dispute with Iran

New York—The most important test for US President Barack Obama
in his efforts to reach peace in the Middle East will not be the test of
intentions, resolve and belief in the ability to achieve the two-state
solution, i.e. to establish the state of Palestine alongside a secure Israel.
The test will lie in the steps the US President will take in seeking peace
between the Arabs and Israel, and in whether these steps will be subjected
to what is merely practical or "feasible," instead of abiding by the clear
and fundamental framework for such a peace, one which enjoys
international consensus as well as sufficient authority and legitimacy.

Indeed, if he fails to assert what must be done and settles for what is
possible, the US President would be jeopardizing the principles necessary
for the solution and a just peace, as he would be exposing the negotiation
process itself to threats that are dangerous and costly for the whole region.
The Obama administration is right to wait until the completion of
important visits by the leaderships of Palestine, Israel and Egypt next
month before putting forth its comprehensive view of the necessary steps
towards peace.

However, the real test for the administration will come before it has
reached a final conclusion and a comprehensive plan, and it will lie in how
it deals with the duality of what is necessary and what is feasible. Indeed,
the framework of negotiations is not balanced, and the tools of
compromise are abundant for Israel and meager for the Palestinians. This
makes the manipulation of what is "feasible" a useful policy for an Israeli
government that does not want the two-state solution and a Palestinian

state, like that of Benjamin Netanyahu, who has thrust Iran into Palestine in a novelty that aims at paralyzing the US President and his commitment to the establishment of a Palestinian state.

Indeed, stopping Iran from pursuing nuclear weapons and restraining its rising regional influence is a stance the Prime Minister of Israel is entitled to put forth and insist upon if he so wishes. However, making such a goal a precondition for engaging in real peaceful negotiations to resolve the Palestinian-Israeli conflict calls for stances from the United States, Russia, Europe and China on parallel yet separate lines: that of thwarting Iran's nuclear ambitions and regional hegemony, and that of exerting serious pressure on Israel so that it would stop maneuvering in the peace process.

Jordanian Monarch King Abdullah II carried this week a message from the Arabs to the US President signifying that a solution to the Palestinian-Israeli conflict is the gateway to resolving all of the region's issues. In other words, Palestine is the gateway to resolving unsettled matters with Iran. Indeed, Tehran uses the Palestinian issue to mobilize support for its ambitions of regional hegemony, in addition to providing practical support to Hamas in Palestine and Hezbollah in Lebanon, rejecting a peaceful solution on the basis of negotiations and rejecting the Arab peace initiative, which is based on accepting Israel and normalizing relations with it in exchange for its withdrawal to the borders of the 1967 defeat and the establishment of a Palestinian state in place of the occupation. If the issue of Palestine remains unresolved, it only benefits the mullahs and revolutionaries in Tehran as well as the forces of extremism, along with the rising forces of anger, which may abandon their dreams of peace due to the clarity of Israel's constant evasion of a peaceful solution.

Barack Obama is convinced that Palestine is a main key to resolving the different issues of the region and will not agree with Benjamin Netanyahu, who aims at freezing peace talks over Palestine until the US efforts to thwart Iran's nuclear and regional ambitions come to fruition. These are spurious stances that could have made this novelty a joke had not the topic been so serious.

(14

النص العربي:

Arabic Text:

أخذ سوريا على محمل الجد

إن سياسة باراك أوباما الجديدة المتعلقة بالتعامل مع سوريا تعتبر تقدما مرحبا به بقوة , و لكنها بحاجة الى أن تتبع حذرا و توازنا أكثر مما هو موجود.

لقد كانت بداية الرئيس جورج بوش – و من غير قصد – جيدة مع سوريا , لكنه فجر الأمور بعد ذلك. في السنة التي تلت هجمات 11 سبتمبر 2001 الإرهابية كانت الحكومة السورية قلقة جدا من أن تقوم الولايات المتحدة الغاضبة بتحويل اتجاه الغضب الى دمشق كما هي الحال مع بغداد.

وفقا لذلك , فإن سوريا التي كانت دائما معادية عقائديا و عديمة الرحمة في قمع التطرف الإسلامي داخل حدودها , قامت بتقديم سيل من المعلومات الحاسمة لواشنطن تتعلق بنشاطات القاعدة في جميع أنحاء الشرق الأوسط. لقد كانت هذه المعلومات ذات قيمة عالية أدت الى تراجع تهديدات القاعدة ضد الولايات المتحدة و الدول الأوروبية الغربية و السعودية و مصر و إسرائيل.

على أي حال , قامت إدارة بوش بالترفع عن سوريا , و رفضت تقديم أي تتازل دبلوماسي أو تجاري مقابل هذه المساعدة , و بدلا من ذلك فقد زادت من انتقادها الغاضب فيما يتعلق بسجل سوريا بحقوق الإنسان و الديمقراطية.

ولهذا و بعد سنة على أحدث 11 سبتمبر قام السوريون الغاضبون و المحبطون بقطع تبادل المعلومات الاستخبارية.

في السنوات التي تلت هذا , لم تقم الحكومة السورية بأي جهد جدي من أجل وقف تدفق المجاهدين المتطوعين و القنابل الشديدة الانفجار و المعدات الأخرى للمتمردين السنة الذين يعملون وسط العراق أسفل وادي الفرات. لقد أثبتت عدم مرونة نهج بوش أنها مكلفة جدا للولايات المتحدة و للقوات المسلحة الأمريكية العاملة في العراق.

إن تعامل الولايات المتحدة مع سوريا تم تجاهله لفترة طويلة على الرغم من أهميته. إن سوريا لا يمكن تجاهلها أو الالتفاف عليها فيما يتعلق بالقضايا الأساسية في السلام العربي–الإسرائيلي و أمن حدود العراق و مستقبل لبنان أو كبح جماح حزب الله , و هو الحزب المدعوم إيرانيا وسوريا في لبنان.

على كل حال , فإن هناك مؤشرات قوية بأن أوباما ووزيرة الخارجية الأمريكية و زملاءهم
قادمون من أجل إحياء المسار السوري بتوقعات غير واقعية و ساذجة في إبعاد سوريا عن
علاقتها القريبة من جمهورية إيران الإسلامية.

النص الإنكليزي:

English Text:
Taking Syria Seriously
The Barack Obama administration's new engagement policy with Syria is a very welcome development, but it needs to be pursued with more caution and balance than may be the case.

Former U.S. President George W. Bush inadvertently actually got off to a good start with Syria, but then he blew it. In the year following the Sept. 11, 2001 terrorist attacks, the Syrian government was greatly concerned that a furious United States might turn its wrath on Damascus as well as Baghdad.

Accordingly, Syria, which has always been ideologically hostile toward and ruthless in suppressing Islamist extremism within its own borders, provided a flood of crucial intelligence to Washington on al-Qaida activities across the Middle East. This Intel was of the greatest value in rolling back al-Qaida threats against the United States, Western European nations, Saudi Arabia, Egypt and Israel.

However, the Bush administration, riding high at the time, refused to grant any diplomatic or trade concessions to Syria in response for this aid, and instead increased their angry criticism of Syria's record on democracy and human rights.

Therefore a year after 9/11, a frustrated and furious Syrian government broke off the intelligence sharing.

In the years that followed, the Syrian government made no serious effort to stop the flow of mujahedin volunteers, high explosives, weapons and other supplies for the Sunni Muslim insurgents operating in central Iraq down the Euphrates valley. The inflexibility of the Bushies therefore proved very costly to the United States and its armed forces operating in Iraq.

A serious U.S. engagement with Syria is long overdue and essential. Syria cannot be ignored or outflanked on the key issues of Israeli-Arab peace, border security for Iraq, the future of Lebanon or the reining in of Hezbollah, the Syrian- and Iranian-backed Party of God in Lebanon.

However, there are already strong indications that Obama, Secretary of State Hillary Clinton and their colleagues are coming to the revived 'Syrian track' with unrealistic and even naïve expectations of 'peeling off' Syria from its close association with the Islamic Republic of Iran.

(15

النص العربي:

Arabic Text:

نملـــك حـــــق الدفـــاع عـــــن أنفسنـــا

كان أكراد العراق حلفاء متحمسين للولايات المتحدة منذ ما قبل اجتياح عام 2003. ولكن مـــع توسيع الأكراد رقعة سيطرتهم على أرضهم الغنية بالنفط، ومع إصرارهم مجددا على المطالبـــة بمدينة كركوك المتنازع عليها، قبيل إجراء استفتاء منصوص عليه دستوريا، تتزايد حدة التـــوتر مع الحكومة المركزية التي يرأسها رئيس الوزراء نوري المالكي ومـــع العـــرب ومجموعـــات عرقية أخرى. أعيد الأسبوع الماضي انتخاب مسعود برزاني رئيسا لحكومة إقلـــيم كردسـتان على الرغم من بروز معارضة شديدة. وبعد أيام من ذلك، جلس مع محـــرر نيوزويـــك لاري كابلو في مجمعه الجبلي المطل من ارتفاع شاهق على مدينة إربيل الكردية. وهـــذه مقتطفـــات:

كيـــــف ينبغـــــي للنـــــاس أن يفـــــسروا نتيجـــــة الانتخـــــاب؟ لقد كان نجاحا لشعب إقليم كردستان. كان شعبنا في الماضي يتعرض للإبادة. أما اليـــوم فبلغنـــا مرحلـــة يـــستطيعون فيهـــا أن ينتخبـــــوا بحريـــة أي شـــخص يرغبـــون فيــه.

كيـــــف ينبغـــــي لنـــــا أن ننظـــــر إلـــى بـــروز معارضـــة جديـــدة؟ أنـــا أرحـــب بهـــا. أرى أن وجـــود معارضـــة هـــو ظـــاهرة صـــحية.

بماذا ترد على الاتهامات بأن الفـــساد مستـــشر جـــدا، وبعـــدم وجـــود ديموقراطيـــة كافيـــة؟ سوف نشكل فورا لجنة استقامة عامة أو لجنة لمكافحة الفساد. وكل شخص لديه أي شـــكوى، أو أي دليـــــل، فهـــــو مـــــدعو للتقـــــدم بهــــا.

للمرة الأولى منذ أشهر عدة، تبادلتما أنت ورئيس الوزراء المالكي الكلام. هل علاقتكما آخـــذة فـــــي التحـــــسن؟ لقد اتصل بي رئيس الوزراء المالكي مهنئا. كانت هذه بادرة جيدة، ونعتقد أنها ستساعد علـــى كـــسر الجليــد.

أدليــت أخيــرا بتــصاريح قاســية حــول مــدى ســوء العلاقــات مــع بغـداد. لقد حصل سوء تفسير لكلامي. في الواقع، بقي موقفي هو نفسه منذ البداية. لم أطالــب لــشعبي بأي شيء آخر أكثر مما يمنحنا إياه الدستور. لطالما قلت إني سأدافع عن حقـوق شـعبنا، وإن الــــــسلاح الوحيــــــد الـــــذي سأســــــتعمله ســــــيكون الدســــــتور.

مــا مــدى قلقــك حيــال انــسحاب الولايــات المتحــدة؟ ضمن الفترة المتبقية، يجب علينا جميعا أن نحل مشاكل العراق. النقطة المهمة هنا هي [الإرادة] السياسية للولايـات المتحـدة وليـس عـدد الجنـود المتبقيـن علـى الأرض. هـل ستغـادر الولايـات المتحدة العراق وتـسمح للوضـع بـأن ينهـار، أم أنهـا ستنــــــسحب بطريقــــــة تخلــــــف وراءهــــــا الاستقــــــرار؟

هل حصل تحسن في العلاقات مـع تركيـا، التـي تُعتبـر مناهضة للطموحـات الكرديـة؟ لقـد حـصل تقـدم لافـت. نحـن نرحـب بـه وسنحاول أن نحـرص علـى تعزيـزه. ماذا عن تعهدك بعدم السماح لحزب العمال الكردستاني بشن هجمات ضد تركيا مـن أراضـي كردســــــتان العراقيــــــة؟ لم نسمح لحزب العمال الكردستاني بشن هجمات من هنا. لقد تم تضخيم حضور الحزب قلـيلا. هذه منطقة جبلية وعرة تقع عند حدود إيران والعراق وتركيا ويصعب على أي قوة أن تــسيطر عليهــــــا.

هل يمكن أن ينتهي المطاف بأن تصبح تركيا حليفة إذا حصل الانسحاب الأمريكي بشكل سيئ؟ بإمكان تركيا أن تلعب دورا إيجابيا في العراق كله. إذا كانت مستعدة للعب دور كهـذا فـنحن جـــــاهزون. ولكــــن لا يمكننـــــا أن نقبــــل التـــــدخل فـــــي شـــــؤوننا الداخليـــــة.

تريد الأمم المتحدة أن تجري تسوية قائمة على التفاوض حول هوية الجهة التي تـسيطر علـى كركــــــوك. هـــــل تؤيــــــد هـــــذه العمليـــــة؟ إجابتي مقتضبة جدا. إن كركوك وأراضي أخرى متنازعا عليها تغطيها مادة في الدستور تنص علــــى خريطــــة طريــــق لحلهــــا. إن أي بــــديل لــــذلك ســــيعقد المــــسألة.

مـــاذا لـــو كنـــت المطالـــب الوحيـــد بـــذلك فيمـــا الآخـــرون يرفـــضونه؟ ستكون حقوق الشعب الكردي قد اغتصبت عندئذ ونحن نملك حق الدفاع عن [أنفسنا] بالوسائل

المت_____و افرة ل_____دينا.

ولك____ن إذا كن___ت تعن___ي الح___رب، فه___م يفوق___ونكم ع___ددا. العدد الأكبر لا يعني الفوز الدائم. [قاعدة] أن الغالبية تحكم هي قاعدة صندوق الاقتراع فق___ط.

النص الإنكليزي:

English Text:
The Right to Defend Ourselves
Iraq's Kurds have been enthusiastic U.S. allies since before the 2003 invasion. But as the Kurds have expanded their control over their oil-rich territory—and as they reassert claims to the contested city of Kirkuk ahead of a constitutionally mandated referendum—tensions are mounting with the central government of Prime Minister Nuri al-Maliki and with Arabs and other ethnic groups. Last week, Massoud Barzani was reelected president of the Kurdistan Regional Government despite a strong opposition showing. Days later, he sat down with NEWSWEEK's Larry Kaplow in his mountain complex high above the Kurdish city of Irbil. Excerpts:

How should people interpret the election?

This was a success for the people of the Kurdistan region. In the past, our people were subject to annihilation. Now we have reached a stage where they can vote freely for whomever they want.

How should we view the emergence of a new opposition?

I welcome it. I see having an opposition as a healthy phenomenon.

What do you say to charges that there is too much corruption, not enough democracy?

We will immediately constitute a public integrity or anticorruption commission. Whoever has any complaint, any evidence, they are welcome to come forward.

For the first time in many months, you and Prime Minister Maliki spoke yesterday. Is your relationship improving?

Prime Minister Maliki called and congratulated me. This was a good initiative, and we believe it will help break the ice.

You have made some tough statements lately about how bad relations are with Baghdad.

There has been misinterpretation of what I said. In fact, my position has been the same from day one. I did not ask for anything else for my people beyond what the Constitution entitles us to. I have always stated that I will defend the rights of our people, and the only weapon in my hand will be the Constitution.

How concerned are you about the U.S. withdrawal?

Within the time that's left, we all have to sort out Iraq's problems. The important thing here is the political [will] of the United States and not the number of troops left on the ground. Will the United States leave Iraq and allow the situation to collapse, or will they withdraw in a way that leaves stability?

Has there been improvement in relations with Turkey, seen as an adversary to Kurdish ambitions?

There has been remarkable progress. We welcome it and we will try to make sure that this progress is sustained.

(16

ترجم النص الآتي إلى الإنكليزية

Translate the following text into English

وسط الاجتماعات

إن التنمية الاجتماعية الاقتصادية للشرق الأوسط بكامله آخذة في الهبوط بـسبب الركـود الذي أصاب عملية السلام التي يجب تنشيطها من جديد. وإذا كان هناك سبيل للخروج من هـذا المأزق فلابد أن يكون على يد كل من العرب والإسرائيليين معاً ، إذ لا يمكن تحقيـق الـسلام عن طريق تقديم جانب واحد للتنازلات بينما يتمسك الطرف الآخر بموقفه.

لم يُظهر الإسرائيليون أى نية لإصلاح الوضع منذ أن انخفضت أعمال العنف بعـد إعـلان الهدنة الأحادية الجانب من قبل الفصائل الفلسطينية قبل ثلاث أسابيع. لقد سمح رئيس الـوزراء الإسرائيلي "آرييل شارون" باستمرار بناء الجدار العازل الذي يحـول الأراضـي الفلـسطينية لسجون مفتوحة تشبه المقاطعات الصغيرة التي تواجدت فـي جنـوب أفريقيـا إبـان الحكـم العنصري، وبذلك سيتم عزل الضفة الغربية وقطاع غزة عن باقي العالم.

(17

ترجم النص الآتي إلى الإنكليزية

Translate the following text into English

نهاية العظمة البريطانية

حتى في العقود التي أعقبت خسارتها لإمبراطوريتها، كانت بريطانيا تتبختر في العـالم وكأنهـا قوة عظمى قزمة. فقوتها الاقتصادية ونفوذها الثقافي، وقوة جيشها النووية وعلاقتها الاستثنائية

بأمريكا ذ كل هذه الأمور ساعدت هذه الدولة الجزيرة الصغيرة على التمتع بنفوذ يفوق حجمهــا الحقيقي. كل هذا يتغير الآن مع استحقاق الفواتير المتأتية من الدور الذي لعبته بريطانيــا فــي الانهيار المالي الذي حصل العام الماضي وفي عملية إنقاذ البنوك والركود الذي أعقب ذلك.

وفجأة، يبدو أن الشمس التي لم تغب قط عن الإمبراطورية البريطانية باتــت تلقــي ظــلالا طويلة على ما تبقى من الطموحات الإمبريالية البريطانية، ويجب على البلد إعادة النظــر فــي دوره في العالم, ربما كبريطانيا صغرى، أو كبريطانيا أقل شأنا بالتأكيد.

هذه لحظة محورية للمملكة المتحدة. فالدين العام في البلد يزداد إلى حد كبير، ولعله سيتضاعف ليصل إلى مستوى قياسي يبلغ 100 بالمائة من الناتج المحلي الإجمالي خلال السنوات الخمــس المقبلة بحسب صندوق النقد الدولي. ويتوقع المعهد الوطني للأبحاث الاقتصادية والاجتماعية أن عودة المدخول الفردي إلى المعدلات التي كان عليها في أوائل عــام 2008 ســتتطلب ســت سنوات. التأثيرات ستطول كل أقسام الحكومة. سيتم تخفيض الميزانيــات فــي وزارة الــدفاع ووزارة الخارجية والكومنولث، مما سيؤثر على قدرة بريطانيا على إظهار قوتهــا العــسكرية والدبلوماسية.

وليس هناك الكثير مما يمكن لرئيس الوزراء غوردن براون أو حكومــة محــافظي ديفيــد كاميرون المقبلة القيام به لعكس هذه النزعة، ذلك إن افترضنا أنهم سيفوزون فــي الانتخابــات العامة التي يجب أن تقام في غضون الأشهر الــ 10 المقبلة. وكما قــال ويليــام هيــغ، نائــب كاميرون ووزير الخارجية في حكومة الظل في خطاب ألقاه حديثا: "ســيصبح أصــعب علــى بريطانيا مع مرور الوقت أن تمارس النفوذ الذي اعتادت على ممارسته على الساحة الدولية."

التاريخ يطبق على بريطانيا لبعض الوقت. فنشوء الاقتصادات العملاقة مثــل الــصين والهنــد لطالما عنى أن دور بريطانيا سيصبح أصغر على طاولة البلدان الأكثر نفوذا في العــالم التــي تزداد ازدحاما. كما أنه عنى أن الولايات المتحدة ستعيد تقييم العلاقة الخاصة المزعومة فيمــا تبحث عن شركاء وتحالفات جديدة، مما سيقلص بالتأكيد دور بريطانيا الكبير بشكل مفرط على الساحة الدولية. سلف براون، توني بلير، قام بمحاولة أخيرة للمحافظة على العظمة البريطانيــة من خلال ما يمكن اعتباره استراتيجية الولاية الــ51: عبر ربط بريطانيا بشكل وثيق بحــروب أمريكا ـــــ على الإرهاب وفي أفغانستان وفي العراق ـــــ وقد اكتسبت لندن أهمية لم تنعم بها منذ أيام تشرتشل والحرب العالمية الثانية.

لكن مهما كانت   الأفضلية التي حظيت بها بريطانيا على المدى القصير، فهي قد زالت بسبب الأضرار السياسية التي ألحقتها بها استراتيجية بلير في الداخل. لقد ازدادت انتقادات المـــواطنين البريطانيين العاديين وحتى أعضاء النظام البريطاني الحاكم لعلاقة لندن الخاضعة لواشنطن فـــي نظرهم. وتضاءل نفوذ بلير، وعانت أجندته السياسية في الداخل نتيجة لذلك، وأصبح واضحا أن بريطانيا لن تتبع أمريكا بشكل تلقائي في المسائل الجيوسياسية.

في الحقيقة، قد يكون بلير أجل الأمر المحتم ليس إلا: فتراجع نفوذ بريطانيـــا هـــو نتيجـــة للأحداث العالمية على غرار التضاؤل النسبي البطيء لنفوذ الولايات المتحدة، التي تجد نفـــسها اليوم في الموقع الذي كانت فيه بريطانيا في أوج مجدها.

(18

ترجم النص الآتي إلى العربية

Translate the following text into Arabic:

Investing in peace

The Palestinian Authority responded to the protest letter sent by 20 prominent Palestinian academics and political leaders, in which they accuse Yasser Arafat of allowing widespread corruption, by jailing most of them. This reflects the executive power of the PA, which has systematically neutralized the legislature as a political force. Past efforts by the elected legislature to enforce accountability and combat corruption have been totally ignored.

This latest incident, quite a serious one (reminiscent of the 1981 arrests in Egypt), comes at a crucial time for Palestinians as peace talks with Israel accelerate and the Palestinian Authority prepares to take on more responsibilities associated with statehood. Indeed, it is precisely now that Arafat needs to consolidate his strength at home and build a broader constituent for peace, because he will have to make unpopular concessions to the Israelis.

What is most intriguing, however, is the position of the United States. The expansion of democracy has been a cornerstone of US foreign policy. Clearly, though, in terms of operational policy, the US position on democracy in the PA is ambiguous. This latest incidence of PA corruption and abuse of power did not even elicit comment from Washington. Why such reluctance? Historical events in the region have disproved the cliché that it is easier to deal with dictatorships than with democratic regimes. No peace will survive if it is not embraced by the people. If the US is serious about peace in Palestine, it would do well to urge the leadership to embrace democracy.

(19

ترجم النص الأتي إلى العربية:

Translate the following text into Arabic:
Bid to upgrade PLO UN Status Qualify Israel's.
The Palestine Liberation Organization (PLO) is seeking to have its U.N status upgraded to a U.N member State, except for the right to vote and stand for election to UN bodies, diplomats said Monday.

It was also planning for an amendment is introduced when the General Assembly approves Israel's UN credential that would stipulate they "do not relate to or cover the occupied Palestinian territory since 1967, including Jerusalem and Syrian Arab Golan".

ثانيا : أخبار اقتصادية ورياضية

Second: Business and Sports News

(1

النص العربي:

Arabic Text:

انقسـام الـعالم إلـى كتلتين
بين الرأسمالية والشيوعية

بعد انتهاء الحرب العالمية الثانية انقسم العالم انقساماً عميقاً إلى كتلتين كبيرتين:

أ‏–   كتلة الدول الرأسمالية, أو النظام الديمقراطي على النمط الغربي.

ب‏–كتلة الدول الاشتراكية, والنظام الشيوعي, أو نظام الديمقراطيات الشعبية.

وتتزعم الكتلة الأولى الولايات المتحدة الأميركية, ويقود الكتلة الثانية الاتحاد السوفياتي.

لم يكن الانقسام طارئاً أو مستغرباً, بل كان متوقعاً وطبيعياً, لأن الخلاف بينهما لم يكن خلاف مصالح وأهواء فقط, بل كان خلافاً أصيلاً عميقاً في المفاهيم السياسية والاقتصادية والاجتماعية لكل من النظامين.

فالنظام الرأسمالي, في جانبه الاقتصادي, يقوم على الملكية الخاصة لموارد الثروة, ويطلق الحرية للأفراد والمشروعات الفردية إلى أوسع مدى, ويؤمن بالربح حافزاً أساسياً إلى التقدم الاقتصادي والاجتماعي, ويقرّ الفروق بين الطبقات.

النص الإنكليزي:

DIVISION OF THE WORLD INTO TWO BLOCS
Between Capitalism and Communism

After the end of Second World War [WWII], the world was profoundly divided into two major blocs:

a- The capitalist bloc, or the democratic system according to the western style.

b- The socialist bloc, and the communist system or popular democracies.

The first bloc is led by the United States of America; the second by the Soviet Union.

The division was neither accidental nor strange, but rather expected and normal; for the difference between them was not only of interests and fancies, but also a deep and genuine one in the political, economical, and social concepts of each of the two systems.

In its economical aspect, the capitalist system is based on the private property of wealth resources. It gives the widestranging freedom to individuals and personal projects, believes in profit as a basic motive for economical and social progress, and acknowledges the differences between classes.

(2

النص العربي:

Arabic Text:

ارتفع العجز التجاري في السلع والخدمات في شهر فبراير إلى 9,71 بليون دولار وهو الأعلى في ست سنوات.

وعزا اقتصاديون هذا الارتفاع بصفة جزئية إلى أن الاقتصاد الأمريكي ينمو بمعدلات أسرع من الدول الصناعية الأخرى ولجوء الولايات المتحدة إلى مزيد من الاستيراد.

النص الإنكليزي:

English Text:
The February trade deficit in goods and services rose to $9.71 billion, the largest in six years.

Economists say this was due in part to the fact that the U.S. economy is growing faster than those of other industrial nations, and thus the U.S.is importing more.

(3

النص العربي:

Arabic Text:

مؤتمر لحماية المستهلكين العرب

تعقد جمعية حماية المستهلك في الإمارات بالاشتراك مع اتحاد المستهلكين العرب مؤتمرا يستمر يومين حول "المستهلك العربي والعولمة".

وقال محمد موسى القاسمي رئيس الجمعية إ الشيخ سلطان بن زايد آل نهيان سوف يفتتح المؤتمر الذي سيعقد في أبوظبي يومي 26 و 27 فبراير.

وذكر الخميس إن المؤتمر سيبحث سبل حماية المستهلكين العرب من المنتجات الخطرة مضيفا إن المؤتمر هو الأول من نوعه الذي يعقد في دولة الإمارات العربية المتحدة، ويشارك فيه ممثلون من كل جمعيات حماية المستهلكين في العالم العربي وبعض الخبراء في القانون والاقتصاد من دول أخرى.

وسوف يناقش المؤتمر أيضا القواعد الموحدة لحماية المستهلكين العرب من التزييف والمنتجات الخطرة وسيقام خلاله معرض للمنتجات الأصلية والمزيفة.

يذكر ان اتحاد المستهلكين العرب أنشىء في أكتوبر من العام الماضي ويضم الأردن وتونس ومصر والإمارات والمغرب والسودان واليمن والجزائر وفلسطين ومقره الرئيسي في الأردن.

النص الإنكليزي:

English Text:
Conference aims to protect Arab consumers
The Emirates Society for Consumer Protection (ESCP), in association with the Arab Consumer Union, will hold a two-day conference on "The Arab Consumer in Globalisation". "Sheikh Sultan bin Zayed Al Nahyan, Deputy Prime Minister of the UAE, will inaugurate the conference, which

will be held in Abu Dhabi from February 26 to 27, 2000," ESCP Chairman Mohammed Mussa Al Kasim said.

He said the conference will seek to protect Arab consumers from dangerous products. The conference is the first of its kind to be held in the UAE. Representatives of all consumer protection societies in the Arab world and some experts on law and economy from other countries will be invited.

The conference will also discuss unified rules to protect Arab consumers against counterfeit and dangerous products. An exhibition of fake and original products will also be held.

The Arab Consumer Union, established in October last year, comprises Jordan, Tunisia, Egypt, The UAE, Morocco, Sudan, Yemen, Algeria and Palestine. Its head office is in Jordan.

(4

النص العربي

Arabic Text:

مناقشة التجارة الحرة

وسط الكثير من الجدل عقدت الجلسة الخامسة بين مصر وتركيا هذا الأسبوع في محاولـــة للاتفاق على اتفاقية التجارة الحرة بين البلدين.

عبر الوفد التركي عن رغبته فى الإسراع بتطبيق فكرة إنشاء منطقة تجـــارة حـــرة مـــع مصر خلال السنوات الثلاث المقبلة. لكن الاتحاد الفيدرالي للصناعات المصرية قال فـــى بيـــان صحفى صدر هذا الأسبوع إن إنشاء منطقة تجارة حرة مع تركيا سيتم على عدة مراحل.

علاوة على ذلك،أكد الاتحاد الفيدرالي للصناعات المصرية أن المنتجـــات المـــذكورة فـــي القائمة التي قدمها لوزير التجارة الخارجية سيتم تأجيل إنتاجها إلى آخر مرحلـــة فـــي الاتفـــاق لتقليل أي أثر سلبي يقع على القطاعات الصناعية التي تنتمي إليها.

وذكر الاتحاد أنه قبل الموافقة على الاتفاق يجب على الفريق المصري القائم بالتفاوض أن يقوم بمزيد من الفحص لسياسة التبادل التجاري مع الخارج ونظم الجمارك في كلتا الدولتين.

وقال الملحق التجاري التركي في القاهرة للصحفيين إن تركيا قامت بالتوقيع بالفعـــل علـــى اتفاقيات ثنائية شبيهة مع 15 دولة أخرى.

وذكر أن هدف الاتفاق مع مصر هو تأسيس نشاط تجاري متوازٍ بـــين الـــدولتين وزيـــادة الاستثمار ذي التمويل الأجنبي، وأضاف أن الأمر بحاجة لفتح خط بحري بين الموانئ التركيـــة والمصرية أيضا.

كان حجم التجارة بين البلدين قد تقلص من 513 مليـون دولار عــام 2001 إلــى 430

مليون دولار عام 2002 .

النص الإنكليزي

English Text:
Free trade debate
AMIDST much controversy, the fifth round of negotiations between Egypt and Turkey was held this week in an attempt to approve a free trade agreement between the two countries.

The Turkish delegation expressed its wish to hasten the application of a free trade area with Egypt during the coming three years. However, the Federation of Egyptian Industries (FEI) in a press release issued this week, argued that a Free Trade Area with Turkey should be a gradual process.

Moreover, the FEI asserted that the products included in a list presented by the FEI to the Ministry of External Trade should be delayed to the last phase of the agreement to minimise any negative impact on these industrial sectors.

The FEI said that before approving the agreement the Egyptian negotiations team should further examine the foreign exchange policy and the customs systems in both countries.

The Turkish commercial attaché in Cairo told reporters that Turkey had already signed similar bilateral agreements with 15 countries.

The aim of an agreement with Egypt is to establish a balance of trade between the two countries and increase foreign-funded investment, he said. The attaché added that a maritime line between Egyptian and Turkish ports was needed as well.

The volume of trade between the two countries declined from "513 million in 2001 to" 430 million in 2002.

(5

النص العربي

Arabic Text:

توصيل خط الغاز الطبيعي

تم تجهيز المرحلة الأولى من عملية إنشاء خط إنتاج الغاز الطبيعي العربي في يونيو

2003، وتم مد خط إنتاج الغاز الطبيعي من مصر للأردن كجزء من خطة تفوق تكلفتها مليار

دولار لمد شبكة إنتاج الغاز الطبيعي بين 4 دول هي مصر، والأردن، ولبنان، وسوريا.

جاء ذلك على لسان وزير البترول المصرى سامح فهمى في تصريح صحفي في

القاهرة عقب اجتماعه مع نظرائه من كل من الاردن وسوريا ولبنان.

ووقع وزراء البترول والطاقة الأربعة أيضاً اتفاقاً لتأسيس الهيئة العربية للغاز ومقرها

بيروت، وتأسيس شركة عربية لنقل وتسويق الغاز ومقرها دمشق، ويمتلك الشركاء الأربعة

نصيبًا متساويًا في إدارة الشركتين الجديدتين.

ومن المفترض أن يمتد خط الغاز من الأردن إلى سوريا عام 2005 ولاحقاً سوف يمتد

إلى لبنان. ويمكن لدول عربية أخرى الاشتراك في المشروع شريطة موافقة الأعضاء الأربعة

المؤسسين.

يدعم المشروع خطة مصر في النهوض بصادراتها من الغاز الطبيعي الذي يقدر

الاحتياطي منه حاليا بأكثر من 1.5مليون متر مربع.

النص الإنكليزي

English Text:
Linking up for gas

OPERATION of the first phase of the Arab natural gas pipeline is set for June 2003. The extension of a natural gas pipeline from Egypt to Jordan is part of a larger '؟؟؟؟1 billion scheme to establish a natural gas grid between four Arab countries - Egypt, Jordan, Syria and Lebanon. The announcement was made in Cairo last week by Egyptian Oil Minister Sameh Fahmy as he met with his Jordanian, Lebanese and Syrian counterparts.

The four oil and energy ministers also signed an agreement to establish the Arab Gas Authority, headquartered in Beirut, and the Arab Gas Transport and Marketing Company, based in Damascus. The four partners are to have joint ownership of the two new bodies.

The pipeline is scheduled to be connected from Jordan to Syria by 2005 and later extended to Lebanon. Other Arab countries may join the project pending approval of the four founding countries.

The project will support Egypt's plans to boost its natural gas exports. Egypt's natural gas reserves arc currently estimated at over 1.5 million cubic meters.

(6

افتتاح مؤتمر الصناعيين في دول مجلس التعاون الخليجي

تحت رعاية الشيخ جاسم بن حمد آل ثاني ولي عهد قطر افتتح في الدوحة اليوم مؤتمر الصناعيين في دول مجلس التعاون الخليجي.

ويعقد المؤتمر الذي يستمر يومين تحت شعار العمالة الوطنية ودورها في التنمية في دول مجلس التعاون الخليجي وتنظمه مؤسسة الخليج للاستشارات الصناعية والأمانة العامة لمجلس التعاون الخليجي ووزارة الطاقة والصناعة والكهرباء والمياه القطرية والغرفة التجارية القطرية.

يرأس الوفد العماني في المؤتمر مقبول بن علي سلطان وزير التجارة والصناعة. ويضم الوفد علي بن مسعود السنيدي وكيل وزارة التجارة والصناعة وعبد العليم بن مستحيل رخيوت رئيس لجنة متابعة ومراقبة التوطين في عمان وحمد بن هاشم الذهب المدير العام للصناعة بوزارة التجارة والصناعة وحمد بن حسن الدهب المدير التنفيذي للمؤسسة العامة للصناعة وعددا من المسؤولين الذين يمثلون الوحدات الحكومية وغرفة تجارة عمان وقطاع الصناعة والأعمال.

وشدد عبدالله بن حمد العطية وزير الطاقة والصناعة والكهرباء والمياه القطري في خطاب ألقاه في افتتاح المؤتمر على أهمية الدور الذي تلعبه العمالة الوطنية في القطاع الصناعي في دول مجلس التعاون الخليجي وقال إن القضايا الصناعية الإقليمية سوف تنال ما تستحقه من اهتمام في المستقبل.

ومن المقرر أن يناقش المؤتمر 15 ورقة عمل حول كيفية إحلال العمالة الوطنية محل العمالة الوافدة في اقتصاديات دول مجلس التعاون الخليجي.

ورأس الجلسة الأولى لمؤتمر الصناعيين السابع عبد العليم بن مستحيل ريخيوت وتم فيها استعراض حاضر ومستقبل العمالة الوطنية في التحول الذي يشهده القطاع الصناعي في دول المجلس.

النص الإنكليزي:

English Text:

AGCC Industrialists Conference Opens

The AGCC's 7th Industrialists Conference opened here today under the auspices of Sheikh Jasim bin Hamad al Thani, Heir Apparent of Qatar.

The two-day meeting is being held under the motto "national Labor and its role in industrial development in the AGCC countries" and jointly organized by the Gulf Organization for Industrial Consultancy, the AGCC Secretariat-General, the Qatari Ministry of Energy, Industry, Electricity and Water and Qatari Chamber of Commerce.

The Omani delegation to the meeting is being headed by Maqbool bin Ali Sultan, Minister of Commerce and Industry and include Ali bin Masud al Sinaidi, Commerce and Industry Undersecretary, Abdul Aalim bin Mustahail Rakhyut, Head of Omanisation follow up and monitoring committee, Hamad bin Hashim al Dhahb, Director –General of Industry at the Ministry of Commerce and Industry, Hamad bin Hassan al Dheeb, Executive Manager of the public Authority for Industrial and a number of officials representing government units, Oman Chamber of Commerce and Industry and the business sector.

In an opening address to the conference, Abdullah bin hamad al Attiya, Qatari Minister of Energy, Industry, Electricity and water stressed the role of national labor in the industrial sector in the AGCC countries. He said regional industrial issues would receive due attention in the future.

The conference will discuss 15 working papers on how to replace expatriates with national labor in the AGCC economies. Meanwhile, Abdul Alim bin Mustahail Rakhyut chaired the first session of the 7th industrialist's conference. The session discussed the present and future of national labor in transforming industries sector in the AGCC countries.

(7

النص العربي:

Arabic Text:

الطيران الإثيوبي يستأنف رحلاته إلى السودان

أعلنت الخطوط الجوية الإثيوبية المملوكة للدولة أمس أنها سوف تستأنف رحلاتها إلى السودان في نوفمبر المقبل بواقع رحلتين أسبوعياً، وذلك بعد توقفها منذ عامين عقب محاولة الاغتيال التي تعرض لها الرئيس المصري حسني مبارك.

وكانت إثيوبيا قد أوقفت رحلاتها الجوية إلى السودان كجزء من العقوبات التي اتخذها ضد حكومة الخرطوم التي اتهمتها بإيواء المسلحين الثلاثة المتهمين بالتورط في المحاولة الفاشلة لاغتيال مبارك في يونيو 1996 أثناء حضوره قمة منظمة الوحدة الأفريقية في أديس أبابا.

وقال كاجنيو فسيا المدير الإقليمي للخطوط الأثيوبية إن الشركة سوف تستأنف رحلاتها بواقع رحلتين أسبوعيا إلى الخرطوم عاصمة السودان في نوفمبر.

من جانبهم ذكر محللون سياسيون في أديس أبابا أن القرار يشير إلى تحسن ملحوظ في العلاقات بين دول القرن الإفريقي.

النص الإنكليزي:

English Text:
Ethiopian Airlines to resume flights to Sudan

State-owned Ethiopian Airlines said yesterday it would resume twice-weekly flights to Sudan in November, two years after they were suspended over an assassination attempt against Egyptian President Hosni Mubarak.

Ethiopia suspended the flights as part of sanctions against the Khartoum government, which it accused of sheltering three gunmen suspected of involvement in an attempt to assassinate Mubarak in June 1996 during an Organization of African Unity summit in Addis Ababa. Mubarak escaped unhurt.

"Ethiopian Airlines will resume its twice-a-week flight to Khartoum, the capital of Sudan, in November," said Kagnew Fesseha, a division manager at Ethiopian Airlines.

Political analysts in Addis Ababa said the decision indicated an improvement in relations between the horns of Africa countries.

(8

النص العربي

Arabic Text:

الاقتصاد الإسلامي كعلم

إن المذهب الاقتصادي الإسلامي لا يزعم لنفسه الطابع العلمي، كالمذهب الماركسي، كمـــا أنه ليس مجرداً عن أي أساس عقائدي معين أو أية نظرة إلى الحياة والكون سوى النفع المادي، كالمذهب الرأسمالي.

وبمعنى آخر، فالاقتصاد الإسلامي ليس علماً مصطنعاً لقوانين يعتبرها طبيعية، وهـــي –

في الواقع- غير طبيعية (الماركسية)، و لا كعلم الاقتصاد السياسي الذي يراقب ويحسب ليقـــدم التفاسير والتعليلات التي لا طائل تحتها (فالتعديلات التي تطرأ عليه كل عام تتجـــاوز الأســـس الثابتة، وتزخر بالتناقضات).

فالاقتصاد الإسلامي هو ثورة لقلب الواقع الفاسد وتحويله إلى سليم. إنه ثورة مـــن داخـــل النفس على النفس الأمارة بالسوء لكي تصبح كريمة سخية عادلة جديرة بصفة الإنـــسان. إنـــه تغيير الواقع، لا وصفه وتفسيره. كما أنه ليس علماً افتراضياً مرسوماً فـــي أروقـــة المكاتـــب، والذي جاءت نتائجه خاطئة وبعيدة جداً عن الواقع.

وما لنا وكلمة العلم في هذا المجال. فلم يسبق في تاريخ الحضارات التليدة التـــي تعاقبـــت على الكون، في عظمتها وجلالها وسموها وعبقريتها، أن ادعت حضارة أن اقتصادياتها كانـــت تقوم على العلم، أو أنها ابتدعت نظريات علمية اقتصادية، خاصة وقد ثبـــت لنـــا أن الاقتـــصاد العلمي، بشقيه الشرقي والغربي، لاقى فشلاً ذريعاً في نظرياته خلال مدة لـــم تتجـــاوز نـــصف القرن، بينما استمر الإسلام ينشر رايته الخيرة، ويسبغ السعادة والرفاهية على الـــشعوب كافـــة قروناً عديدة.

النص الإنكليزي

English Text:
The Islamic Economy as a Science
The Islamic doctrine in economy does not claim to be a scientific one like Marxism, it is not void of a religious ground, and it is not restricted to a certain outlook to life especially the material benefit like capitalism. In other words, Islamic economy is not a science with established principles and rules that are considered natural, but in fact unnatural at all like Marxism, and it is not a political-economic science that presents observations, reasons and statistics that are futile (as they are liable to change every year an could be very contradictory).

The Islamic economy is a revolution to change the corrupted circumstances and to rectify it, it is a revolution from within the self against the evil aspect of the self to be a generous, just self, worthy of the human being. It is a change of current circumstances, not just a mere description or interpretation of it. It is not also a hypothetical branch of science to be restricted to bookshelves, as science is liable to faults and could be away from reality.

The Islamic economy is not a science. We do not find in the history of past civilizations that have appeared in the world in their splendor, grandeur, and ingenuity, that they have claimed that their economy has been based on a branch of science, Or that they have developed a scientific theory of economy, especially that it has been proven that scientific economy with its oriental and occidental aspects, has failed totally with its theories within 50 years, whereas Islam is still spreading its happiness, prosperity, and goodness on many peoples through many centuries.

(9

النص العربي

Arabic Text:

أوروبا في حالة إنكار بشأن عمق أزمتها

هل تتصرف أوروبا على مستوى الخطر الذي يهدد الاقتصادي العالمي ؟ يقول الخبراء إنه بعد الاندفاعة الأولية لصانعي السياسة الأوروبيين في الخريف الماضي أخذوا الآن يتحركون ببطء مما لا يساعدهم على مواكبة الوضع المتردي , كما أنهم لا يبدون استعدادا لتقديم رزمة تحفيز ضخمة على الطريقة الأمريكية , أو لمحاكاة خطوات السياسة النقدية غير التقليدية التي تقوم بها بريطانيا , بما في ذلك شراء سندات الشركات والسندات الحكومية للمساعدة على إنعاش الإقراض.

وفي هذا الصدد يقول توماس ماير من دويتشه بانك في بريطانيا: "إنهم في حالة إنكار , ويأملون أن يأتي شيء ما من الولايات المتحدة لمساعدتهم. النظام الأوروبي ليس مصمما لاتخاذ الإجراءات غير التقليدية المطلوبة حاليا".

ولم يعد الخبراء الاقتصاديون الخاصون وحدهم الذي يشتكون من الحذر الأوروبي. فقبل أيام بدا أن الرئيس أوباما ووزير خزانته تيموثي غايثنر يوجهان الانتقادات للاوروبيين قبل اجتماع وزراء المالية وحكام المصارف المركزية لمجموعة العشرين , وهو آخر اجتماع رئيسي قبل القمة المقررة لزعماء هذه الدول يوم 2 ابريل. وقال أوباما: " أعتقد أنه من المهم جدا أن يفهم الشعب الأمريكي أنه بالرغم من هجومية الإجراءات التي اتخذناها حتى الآن فإن من المهم جدا أن نضمن تحرك دول أخرى في الاتجاه ذاته؛لأن الاقتصاد العالمي مترابط" . وأضاف غايثنر: "كل ما نفعله في الولايات المتحدة سيكون أكثر فعالية إذا ما تحرك العالم معنا".

ولا تزال جهود التحفيز الأوروبية تشكل جزءا صغيرا من حجم الرزمة الأمريكية المماثلة.

ويقدر ماير أن الرزمة الأمريكية من الإنفاق الجديد والتخفيضات الضريبية التي ستمول بالعجز على مدى عامين تعادل نحو 6% من إجمالي الناتج المحلي السنوي الأمريكي. وفي

المقابل تعادل رزمة الإنقاذ الألمانية للفترة ذاتها 2.6%, وفي منطقة اليورو تعادل 1-1.5 %

فقط من إجمالي ناتجها المحلي.

النص الإنكليزي:

English Text:

After a burst of initial action last autumn, experts say policy makers on the Continent are moving too slowly to keep up with the worsening situation, unwilling to ante up for a big U.S.-style stimulus package or emulate unconventional monetary policy moves now under way in Britain, including buying up corporate and government bonds to help revive lending.

"They are in denial, and hoping that something from the U.S. will come along to help them out," said Thomas Mayer, chief European economist in London for Deutsche Bank. "The European system isn't designed for taking the unconventional policy measures that are now needed."

And it is no longer just private economists who are complaining about European caution. On Wednesday, President Barack Obama and his Treasury secretary, Timothy Geithner, appeared to turn up the heat ahead of this weekend's meeting of Group for 20 finance ministers and central bankers outside London, the last major meeting before the scheduled summit meeting of world leaders on April 2.

"I think it's very important for the American people to understand that as aggressive as the actions we are taking have been so far, it's very important to make sure that other countries are moving in the same direction, because the global economy is all tied together," Obama said. Geithner added, "Everything we do in the United States will be more effective if we have the world moving with us."

So far, European stimulus efforts are only a fraction of the size of the comparable American package.

Mayer estimates Washington's recently approved package of deficit-financed new spending and tax cuts, which is concentrated in the next two years, equals about 6 percent of the annual U.S. gross domestic product. That stands in contrast to 2.6 percent for Germany over a comparable period. Within the euro zone, the average stimulus equals 1 percent to 1.5 percent of GDP.

(10

العالم مهدد بخطر المجاعة

باتريك سيل

يعاني أكثر من بليون شخص يومياً من الجوع, أي سدس سكان العالم البالغ عددهم 6.5 بليون نسمة. ولا يعاني هؤلاء الجوع من وقت إلى آخر فحسب, بل يعانونه بصورة مُزمنة. فهم غير قادرين على إيجاد الغذاء الكافي لإطعام أولادهم أو لسدّ احتياجاتهم الخاصة. وعددهم يتزايد باستمرار.

لكن ما الذي يفعله العالم حيال هذا الموضوع؟ الجواب هو أنه يفعل القليل.

تعتبر المشكلة كبيرةً جدا ومنتشرة بشكل واسع. كما أنها, بطريقة أو بأخرى, تسير ببطء إلى حدّ يمنع حكومات البلدان الغنية من إعطائها الأولوية التي تستحقها. لم تظهر مسألة الجوع في العالم على لائحة المسائل الرئيسية التي تثير مخاوف مجموعة الدول العشرين, خلال القمة الأخيرة التي عُقدت في لندن.

وبدأ البعض يدرك أن مشكلة الأمن الغذائي تشكّل خطراً كبيراً على الاستقرار العالمي. فأقرّ وزراء الزراعة في مجموعة البلدان الصناعية الثماني, الذين اجتمعوا في إيطاليا في نهاية الأسبوع, بفداحة المشكلة. وتعهّدوا بالاستمرار في مكافحة الجوع. لكن باستثناء المطالبة بزيادة الاستثمارات العامة والخاصة في ميدان الزراعة, لم يذكر البيان الختامي الصادر عن الاجتماع الوزاري أي اقتراحات جديدة. وتمثّل الخبر السار الوحيد في إعلان إدارة أوباما أنّها ستضاعف المساعدة الأمريكية الخاصة بالزراعة في البلدان الفقيرة لتبلغ بليون دولار أمريكي في السنة المقبلة.

وعلى هامش الاجتماع في إيطاليا, قال وزير الزراعة الأمريكي توم فيلساك لصحيفة «فاينانشل تايمز»: «لا يتعلق الموضوع بالأمن الغذائي فحسب, بل بالأمن القومي والأمن البيئي». وأضاف: «يجب أن تصبح هذه المسألة مسألةً أساسيةً ومركزيةً في النقاشات الدولية». لكن رغم هذه الأقوال الجريئة, لم تبرز أي إشارة تدل على تحرك منسّق قد تقوم به مجموعة البلدان الصناعية الثمانية.

اطّلع الوزراء على تقرير حضّرته الرئاسة الإيطالية , وحذّر من أنّ تجنّب الجوع المدقع رهن بمضاعفة الإنتاج الزراعي العالمي بحلول العام 2050, عندما سيصل عدد سكان العالم إلى 9 بلايين نسمة. ودعا التقرير إلى «التدخل فوراً», غير أنه لم يتمّ اقتراح أي تحرك فوري.

عندما ارتفعت أسعار السلع الزراعية بين العامين 2007 و2008, اهتزّ نحو ثلاثين بلداً, من هاييتي إلى مصر وبنغلادش, نتيجةً لأعمال الشغب الناجمة عن أزمة الغذاء. وارتفعت الهجرة غير الشرعية إلى أوروبا من المغرب وأفريقيا جنوب الصحراء, وهما منطقتان تلقّتا ضربة قاسية بفعل الارتفاع الحاد في أسعار الغذاء. واستحوذت أعمال القرصنة التي شهدتها السواحل الصومالية على انتباه العالم, غير أن عدداً قليلاً من الناس أقرّ بأن جذور هذا الواقع تعود إلى ظاهرة الفقر.

وعند ارتفاع موجة الذعر الغذائي السنة الماضية, فرضت البلدان الرائدة في تصدير المواد الغذائية كالهند والأرجنتين قيوداً على المبيعات في الدول الأجنبية. لكنّ ذلك لم يؤد إلا إلى تعطيل الأنماط التجارية القائمة, وإلى تأجيج مخاوف البلدان المستوردة.

تكمن عوامل متعدّدة وراء تفاقم الجوع في دول العالم, بما فيها الارتفاع الملحوظ في عدد سكان العالم الذي يُقال إنه يرتفع بواقع 80 مليون نسمة سنوياً, والنقص في المياه والأراضي الصالحة للزراعة, خاصةً في المناطق الجافة في الشرق الأوسط, فضلاً عن التقلّبات العالية في أسعار الأغذية, والقيود المالية التي تمنع بعض الحكومات من مواصلة دعم أسعار الأغذية وفق المستويات السابقة, ورحيل الشباب عن الأراضي, إضافةً إلى عامل جديد ومخيف وغير قابل للقياس, ألا وهو تغيّر المناخ.

تعتبر منظمة الأغذية والزراعة في الأمم المتحدة أن ضخ 30 بليون يورو سنوياً في مجال الزراعة العائلية في شتّى أنحاء العالم قد يساهم في ضبط ظاهرة الجوع, وقد يؤول حتى إلى عكس مسارها. غير أن نداء منظمة الأغذية والزراعة لم يجد آذناً مصغية.

ولما كان من غير المرجّح أن تقدم قوى العالم على أي تحرك جماعي, فإن البلدان التي تملك الوسائل المطلوبة تعمد إلى الاستعانة بالدول الأجنبية لمعاجلة مشكلة الأمن الغذائي, وذلك عبر شراء مساحات شاسعة من الأراضي الصالحة للزراعة خارج حدودها أو استئجارها.

النص الإنكليزي

English Text:
The Global Threat from Hunger
Patrick Seale

Over one billion people go hungry every day—that is to say, one sixth of the world's population of 6.5 billion. They are not just hungry from time to time. They are chronically hungry. They can never find enough food to feed their children or meet their own needs. Their number is growing.

What is the world doing about it? The answer is: very little.

The problem is too big, too widespread and—and also, in a sense, too slow moving—for rich countries to give it the priority it deserves. World hunger did not feature among the top concerns of the G-20 at their recent summit meeting in London.

Yet, it is beginning to be realised that food insecurity poses a threat to global stability. Meeting in Italy last weekend, agriculture ministers of the G8 industrialised countries recognised the extent of the problem. They pledged to continue fighting hunger. But beyond calling for increased public and private investment in agriculture, the final communiqué was short on fresh proposals. The only good news was the announcement by the Obama Administration that it would double US aid to agriculture in poor countries to $1bn next year.

In the wings of the meeting in Italy, the U.S. agriculture secretary tom Viilsack told the Financial Times. 'This is not just about food security. This is about national security. It is about environmental security. "The issue, he said, should become" an issue that is front and central in international discussions. In spite of these bold words, there was no sign of concerted action by the G8 countries.

The ministers were given a report by the Italian presidency which warned that, if widespread starvation was to be avoided, global agricultural output had to double by 2050—when the world's population would reach a staggering 9 billion. The report called for "immediate interventions." But nothing immediate was suggested.

When prices of agricultural commodities surged in 2007-2008, some thirty countries—from Haiti to Egypt to Bangladesh—were shaken by food riots. Illegal migration to Europe increased from the Maghreb and sub-Saharan Africa. Piracy off the Somali coast captured the world's attention, but few were prepared to recognise that its roots lay in poverty.

Many diverse factors lie behind the world-wide increase in hunger. They include a soaring world population, which is said to be increasing by 80 million a year; a shortage of water and arable land, notably in the dry Middle East; highly volatile food prices; financial constraints which prevent some governments from continuing to subsidise food prices at former levels; a flight of young people from the land; and—that new and terrifying imponderable—climate change.

The UN's Food and Agricultural Organisation (FAO) estimates that an injection of 30 billion Euros a year into family farming across the world could hold hunger in check, and even reverse it. But the FAO appeal has largely fallen on deaf ears.

As collective action by world powers is unlikely, countries with the means to do so are outsourcing the problem of food security by buying or leasing vast tracts of arable land outside their borders.

(11

النص العربي:

Arabic Text:

لماذا يتردد الاوروبيون في مجاراة رزم الانقاذ الأمريكية؟

تستخدم كلمة " اوروبا " في السياسة الأمريكية أحيانا للدلالة على " الحكومة الكبيرة" او الدور الكبير للحكومة في حياة الشعب . ولذلك وفي خضم ركود عالمي ومع انفاق الولايات المتحدة والصين لتريليونات الدولارات من اجل التحفيز المالي , من الطبيعي أن نتوقع من الحكومات الاوروبية انفاقا محموما ايضا . الحقيقة هي ابعد ما تكون عن ذلك . ففي حين تكرس الولايات المتحدة نحو ٦ في المئة من اجمالي ناتجها المحلي للتحفيز المالي نجد ان فرنسا والمانيا تتفقان مبالغ زهيدة, في حدود ٢٦ مليار يورو للأولى و٥٠ مليارا للثانية . وبينما تأمل الولايات المتحدة أن تؤدي قمة الدول العشرين المقبلة الى الاتفاق على رزمة تحفيز عالمية يوجه صانعو السياسة الاوروبيون تحذيرات من اخطار الانفاق الحكومي المفرط . وفي حين كان الاحتياطي الاتحادي يغرق الاقتصاد الأمريكي بالأموال كان البنك المركزي الاوروبي يكتفي بخفض اسعار الفائدة ببطء وعلى مضض .

هذا الموقف الاوروبي اثار انتقادات كثيرة , وقال الخبراء ان السياسيين الاوروبيين غافلون عن خطورة الأزمة . قد يكون في هذا الاتهام شيء من الحقيقة, ولكن الحذر الاوروبي يعكس ايضا فروقا مهمة بين الاقتصادين الاوروبي والأمريكي , كما يعكس موقفا مختلفا بشكل جذري ازاء امور مثل التضخم والديون . واذا بدا ان صانعي السياسة

الاوروبيـــــــــين والأمريكيين, في تصريحاتهم العلنية, يتعاملون مع أزمتـــــــــين ماليتين مختلفتين تمامـــــــــا فهذا لأنهمـــــــــا بمعنى ما مختلفتان بالفعل .

من جهة البلدان الاوروبية اكبر تأثير على السياسة لم يطحنها هذا الركود, وفـــــــــي بلدان مثل ايرلندا واسبانيا حيث انفجرت فقاعات مســـــــــاكن هائلة كانت العواقب جسيمة, اما في المانيا حيث لم تكن هناك فقاعة فان عددا أقل من الناس يعانون من الديون او يرون ثرواتهم وهي تتلاشى .

صحيح ان الاقتصاد الالماني الذي يعتمد بقوة على الصادرات ليس في افضل حال, ويبدو انـــــــــه معرض للانكماش هذا العام اكثر مـــــــــن الاقتصاد الأمريكي . ولكن معدل البطالة في المانيا ارتفع بنسبة اقل من ارتفاعه في الولايات المتحدة . والواقع ان فقدان الوظائف في معظم اوروبا كان اقل حدة مما في الولايات المتحدة لأسباب منها ان معـــــــــدل البطالة كان مرتفعا جدا في الاصل . فقد ارتفع معدل البطالة الأمريكي بنحو ٪ ٣ منذ يناير ٢٠٠٨ ولكنه بالكاد ارتفع بنسبة ٪ ١ في اوروبا .

النص الإنكليزي:

English Text:

In American politics, "Europe" is usually a code word for "big government." So in the midst of a global recession, with the U.S. and China shelling out trillions in fiscal stimulus, you might expect that European governments would be spending furiously too, Far from it. While the U.S. is devoting almost six per cent of its G.D.P. to fiscal stimulus, France and Germany are spending a barely noticeable twenty-six billion euros and fifty billion euros, respectively. Whereas the U.S. hopes that the upcoming G20 summit will lead to a global stimulus package, European policymakers have been warning against the dangers of "crass Keynesianism." The U.S. Federal Reserve has been flooding our economy with money, but the European Central Bank has cut interest rates slowly and reluctantly. Far from wild-eyed leftists, Europeans are looking downright conservative.

Europe's response has earned it plenty of criticism, with pundits arguing that its politicians are oblivious of the seriousness of the crisis. There may be some truth in this charge, but Europe's caution also reflects important differences between its economy and ours, as well as a profoundly different attitude toward things like inflation and debt. If European and American policymakers seem, in their public statements, to be dealing with two very different financial crises, it's because, in some sense, they are.

To begin with, the biggest European countries, which have the most influence on policy, have not been crushed by this recession. In countries like Ireland and Spain, where huge housing bubbles burst, the devastation has been immense. But in Germany, where there was no bubble, fewer people are struggling with debt or watching their wealth go up in smoke. To be sure, Germany's economy, which is heavily dependent on exports, is not in good shape; it looks set to shrink more this year than the U.S. economy. But the unemployment rate in Germany has risen much less than it has here. Indeed, in most of Europe job losses have been less severe, in part because unemployment was already quite high. The U.S. unemployment rate has risen nearly three percentage points since January, 2008. Europe's is up barely one per cent.

(12

النص العربي:

Arabic Text:

إلى أي مستوى يمكن أن تنخفض أسعار الكمبيوتر الشخصي؟

عندما اشترى " جيم وول" أول حاسوب شخصي عام ١٩٩٥ دفع ثمنـــــــــه ٢٥٠٠ دولار . . وفي ديسمبر الماضي اشترى حاسوبا محمولا لابنته مقابل ٦٠٠ دولار فقط . ويقول وول : " في السابق كان شراء حتسوب قرارا اكبر بكثير اما اليوم فإن إطارات سيارتي تكلـــــــــف أكثر مـــــــــن حاسوبي المحمول".

بالطبع اسعار الحواسيب الشخصية تميل الى الانخفاض بمرور الزمن, لكنها شهدت في الأشـــــــهر القليلة الماضية تراجعا أكثر حدة بكثير من نسبة ٥ ٪ السنوية المألوفة للانخفاض . وخـــــــلال الربع الأخير من عام ٢٠٠٨ انخفض متوسط سعر الحاسوب الشخصي بنسبة . . ٣ ١٤,٪ ولم يســـــــبق للأسعار ان تراجعت بســـــــرعة اكبر إلا مرة واحدة خلال الأعوام الـــ ١٥ الماضية, وكان ذلك في الربع الاخير مـــــــن ٢٠٠١ مع انفجار فقاعة اسهم الانترنت الذي أدى الى انخفاض بنسبة . . ١٤,٥ ٪ وقد يكون الانحدار الاخير نذيرا بانحـــــــدارات مقبلة اكثر حدة . فمع لجوء المســـــــتهلكين الى تخفيض إنفاقهم بســـــــبب الازمة ــ الاقتصاديــــة العالمية ومع تزايد شعبية الحواسيب الرخيصـــــــة التكلفة المعروفة بالحواسيب الدفترية, يمكن لصناعة الحواسيب ان تشهد انخفاضا كبيرا في الاسعار . ويتوقـــــــع احـــــــد المحللـــــــين انخفاضا في اسعار

الحاسوب المحمول المتوسط بنسبة ١٠ % هذا العام وبنسبة ١٥ % للحاسوب المكتبي .

هذا التراجع المتسارع للاسعار يمكن ان يبدل طبيعة صناعة الحواسيب . انه في مصلحة المستهلكين والشركات الذين يحصلون على طاقة حاسوبية أعظم من السابق مقابل اقل من ١٠٠٠ دولار في اغلب الأحيان وحتى بسعر ٢٥٠ دولارا للحاسوب الدفتري .

ولكن هذا الانخفاض مؤلم لشركات التكنولوجيا . وتواجه شركات صناعة الحواسيب مثل " دل " و " لينوفو " مصاعب مع بحث الزبائن عن ارخص الاسعار . وفي الوقت ذاته يشعر مصنعو مكونات الحاسوب مثل شرائح الذاكرة والشاشات بضغوط مماثلة . وايضا الشركتان الأقوى في مجال الحاسوب الشخصي " انتل " و " مايكروسوفت " تقومان بتعديلات على استراتيجياتهما للتعامل مع الواقع الجديد لهذه وينـدوز للحاسوب الدفتري أي اقل من نصف الثمن الذي تتقاضاه الشركة عن ارخص نسخة من ويندوز اكس بي لاجهزة الحاسوب المحمول . ويصف احد المحللين الحاسوب الدفتري بأنه " منحى مزعج " بالنسبة لمايكروسوفت . ويمكن لاجهزة الحواسيب الشخصية الارخص ان تنشط الطلب خصوصا من الزبائن الجدد . وبالرغم من الكساد الاقتصادي هنالك توقعات بأن تزداد شحنات الحاسوب الشخصي لهذا العام بنسبة ١٢ % ليصل عددها عالميا الى ١٦٥ مليون وحدة . والواقع ان بعض صانعي الحاسوب الشخصي سيكونون سعداء في هذه الظروف ببيع أي شيء حتى الحاسوب الدفتري الرخيص الثمن للتعويض عن تراجع مبيعات الحاسوب الشخصي الاغلى ثمنا . وتتوقع شركة " سي تي ال " الأمريكية التي تبيع نحو ١٠٠ ألف حاسوب سنويا ان تشكل الاجهزة الدفترية نصف مبيعاتها هذا العام بعد ان كانت ٣٠ % في ٢٠٠٨ . ويقول احد مسؤوليها ان الاجهزة الدفترية تبيع بسهولة اكبر وانه ليس بالإمكان مقاومة هذا الاتجاه ولذلك لابد من التكيف معه . الصناعة . ومن المؤكد ان الركود يشكل عاملا رئيسيا في تراجع اسعار الحاسوب الشخصي ولكن هذه الاسعار ستتعافى في وقت ما بالرغم من الوضع الحالي المتردي للاقتصاد . ولكن الشيء الذي قد لا يتبدل هو الاهمية المتزايدة للحاسوب الدفتري . وخلال العام الماضي كانت شركات مثل " أسوس" و " ايسر " تنتج بكثرة الاجهزة المبسطة التي تتراوح أسعارها عادة بين ٣٠٠ و ٦٠٠ دولار.

ومع تهافت المستهلكين على هذه المنتجات بادرت " هيوليت باكارد " وشركات رئيسية اخرى الى طرح حواسيبها الدفترية .

ويقـــــــال انه حتى " أَبل " تفكر في طرح جهاز من هذا النوع . ومـــــــن المتوقع ان يتضاعف عـــــــدد الحواسيب الدفترية المشحونة هذا العام ليشكل ٪ ١٥ من إجمالي شحنات الحاسوب الشخصي .

English Text:

How Low Can PC Prices Go?

When Jim Wahl bought his first computer back in 1995, it cost $2,500. In December, when the Dallas acquisitions manager bought laptop for his daughter, he paid just $600. "[In the past], it was a lot bigger decision," Wahl says. "But now, the tires on my car cost more than my laptop."

Personal computer prices tend to fall over time, of course. But in the past few months, computer prices have plummeted much more sharply than the usual 5% yearly declines. In the fourth quarter of 2008 alone, the average personal computer's selling price dropped 14.3%, according to consultancy IDC. Only once in the past 15 years have PC prices declined at a faster rate—in the fourth quarter of 2001, as the Internet bubble burst, when they dipped 14.5%, according to IDC.

And the recent slide may be a precursor to sharper declines ahead. As consumers cut back amid the global economic downturn and the popularity of low-cost computers known as netbooks rises, the computer industry could see a big drop in prices. "We are not done yet," says Rob Enderle, president of consultant Enderle Group. "The drop is going to continue through the year." Matthew Wilkins, an analyst with researcher iSuppli, predicts that average laptop prices could fall a further 10% in 2009, while desktop prices drop 15%.

The accelerating price declines could change the dynamics of the tech industry. For consumers and corporate customers, the trend is overwhelmingly favorable. They get more computing capability than ever before, often for less than $1,000 and, in the case of netbooks, for as little as $250.

But for tech companies, the squeeze is painful. Computer makers such as Dell (DELL) and Lenovo are struggling as customers hunt hard for bargains. Manufacturers of components like memory chips and monitors are feeling the pinch, too. Even Intel (INTC) and Microsoft (MSFT), the two most powerful companies in the personal computer business, are making strategic adjustments to address the new realities of the business. The recession is certainly a major factor in the PC price declines, and, as rough as the economy looks now, it will recover at some point. What may not change, however, is the growing importance of netbooks. Manufacturers like Asus and Acer have been rolling out the stripped-down devices, which typically run \$300 to \$600, over the past year. And as consumers have scooped the products up, Hewlett-Packard and other top manufacturers have weighed in with their own netbooks. Even Apple (AAPL) is reportedly considering coming out with one of the devices. The number of netbooks shipped this year is expected to double, to 20 million, according to IDC, reaching 15% of all portable PC shipments.

(13

النص العربي

Arabic Text:

ما هو سر النهضة الصناعية في المغرب العربي ؟

بعد سقوط جدار برلين انضمت شركة سوميتومو اليابانية للصناعات الكهربائية إلى عدد كبير من شركات تزويد صناعة السيارات بإنشاء مصانع منخفضة التكلفة على الحافة الشرقية لأوروبا. وأقامت الشركة مصانع لها من بولندا إلى بلغاريا وهي تمتلك اليوم أكثر من عشرة مصانع في المنطقة. ولكنها تعمل الآن على نقل انتاجها إلى الجنوب من اوروبا , وبالذات إلى مدينة طنجة القديمة , و الى بو سلام وهي بلدة تجارية تقع وسط حقول القمح شمال تونس. وتقول الشركة انه مع ارتفاع التكاليف في اوروبا الشرقية اصبح تحقيق الارباح أكثر صعوبة. وعلى النقيض من ذلك يوفر شمال افريقيا اجورا اقل بكثير وأعدادا وفيرة من العمال المتحمسين.

وليست سوميتومو الشركة الوحيدة التي تتوجه الى المغرب العربي , وهو مجموعة من اربعة بلدان نامية على الساحل الجنوبي للمتوسط. وتجتذب المنطقة بقيادة المغرب وتونس وبعدد سكانه البالغ 84 مليونا استثمارات مهمة تجاوزت 30 مليار دولار خلال الأعوام الخمسة الماضية وذلك في مجالات تمتد من مصانع السيارات والطيران إلى منتجعات الخمس نجوم.

وحتى الجزائر وليبيا اللتان كانتا منبوذتين على المسرح الدولي اخذتا تنعشان اقتصاديهما الراكدين , وتفتحان ابوابهما أمام الاستثمارات الأجنبية . وبعد إنشاء خط انابيب تحت المتوسط اصبحتا مزودتين رئيسيتين بالغاز الطبيعي لأوروبا التي تبحث عن بدائل لروسيا غير المستقرة سياسيا.

ومن المرجح أن تواصل هذه البلدان نموها بالرغم من الأزمة الاقتصادية العالمية. وتتراوح تنبؤات النمو لعام 2009 بين 3.7% في تونس وأكثر من 5% في ليبيا. ويصنف مكتب "يولر هيرمز" الاستشاري لمخاطر الاستثمار كلا من تونس والمغرب على انهما أكثر أمانا من هنغاريا ورومانيا وبلغاريا.

إن جاذبية بلدان المغرب العربي واضحة , فهي تقع في الباحة الخلفية للقارة الاوربية , وتبعد طنجة 8 اميال فقط عن اسبانيا عبر مضيق جبل طارق. وتنعم حكومات المنطقة باستقرار نسبي وببيئة مشجعة للاستثمارات. كما انها رخيصة حيث تتراوح اجور عمال المصانع بين 195 و 325 دولارا في الشهر , مقارنة باجر شهري متوسط يبلغ 671 دولارا تدفعه شركة رينو في مصنعها لانتاج سيارات "داسيا لوغان" في رومانيا.

وتساعد هذه الأرقام على تفسير سبب شروع رينو بإنشاء مصنع تجميع في طنجة سيكون أكبر مصانعها. ومن المتوقع ان يستخدم المصنع 6000 عامل , ويقول مسؤولون في المغرب أنه يمكن ان يجتذب مزودين بحيث يوفر فرص عمل إضافية لنحو 35 ألف شخص. وبالرغم من أن الازمة العالمية أخرت تدشين المصنع مدة تصل إلى العام فإن كارلوس غصن مدير رينو يقول إن الشركة ملتزمة بالمشروع الذي سينتج سيارات "لوغان" رخيصة التكلفة لبلدان المغرب العربي ولغيرها.

وتبدي صناعة الطيران الاوروبية تفاؤلا مماثلا بالمنطقة. فمن المقرر أن تفتتح شركة ايرباص في العام المقبل مصنعا في تونس بتكلفة 76 مليون دولار سيوظف 1500 عامل. وفي الوقت الحاضر تستخدم الشركات المزودة لهذه الصناعة أكثر من 10 آلاف عامل في المغرب لصناعة صفائح هياكل الطائرات والانابيب ذات الضغط العالي وغيرها. وعلى سبيل المثال تمتلك مجموعة "سافران" الفرنسية ستة مصانع في المغرب تستخدم نحو 1400 شخص. وفي مصنعها الحسن الاضاءة والذي يوحي بالانشراح بالقرب من مطار الدار البيضاء تعمل نساء في سترات بيضاء في لف أسلاك كهربائية لتحويلها إلى كيبلات مخصصة لطائرات بوينغ وايرباص. ويستخدم هذا المشروع المشترك لبوينغ والخطوط الملكية المغربية 600 شخص يتقاضون في المتوسط 315 دولارا في الشهر. ويبلغ عدد ساعات العمل الاسبوعية 44 ساعة أي اكثر مما هي عليه في معظم البلدان الأوروبية. ونظرا لعدم وجود اتحادات عمالية فإن المديرين يجدون سهولة في الملاءمة بين الانتاج والطلبات عن طريق تكليف العمال بساعات عمل إضافية.

وتعد الدار البيضاء نموذجا لحيوية بلدان المغرب. فهي مدينة تعج بالحركة ويبلغ عدد سكانها 4 ملايين, حيث تطل الأبراج المكتبية على المدينة القديمة بشوارعها الضيقة والمتعرجة. وعند أطراف المدينة يضع العمال اللمسات النهائية على مجمع هائل للمباني المكتبية. وسيضم المجمع مكاتب اتصالات وعمليات لشركات مثل بي ان بي باريباس الفرنسي وبنك بي ان بي باريباس الفرنسي وذلك رغبة منها بالاستفادة من مهارات اللغة الفرنسية في المغرب.

ويتمثل عنصر الجذب الآخر في اليد العاملة الماهرة وذلك بفضل التركيز على التعليم في المغرب وتونس. ويصنف المنتدى الاقتصادي العالمي تونس في المرتبة السابعة في العالم من

حيث جودة تعليم الرياضيات والعلوم (بينما تأتي الولايات المتحدة في المرتبة 48). وافتتح المغرب جامعة على النمط الأمريكي في جبال أطلس حيث يجري التعليم باللغة الانكليزية ويتوقع من الطلبة تمضية فصل دراسي واحد على الأقل في الخارج.

النص الإنكليزي:

English Text:
Manufacturing: The Rise of the Maghreb
Casablanca/Algiers - After the fall of the Berlin Wall, Japan's Sumitomo Electric Industries joined a crowd of automotive suppliers setting up low-cost plants on Europe's eastern rim. It opened factories from Poland to Bulgaria and today has a dozen facilities in the region. But now, Sumitomo is shifting production south of Europe—to the ancient Moroccan port of Tangier and to Bou Salem, a market town set among wheat fields in northern Tunisia. As costs rise in Eastern Europe, the company says, it's getting harder to make a profit. North Africa, by contrast, offers far lower wages and plenty of eager workers.

Sumitomo isn't the only company beating a path to the Maghreb, a swath of four developing countries along the Mediterranean's southern shore. Led by Morocco and Tunisia, the region of 84 million people is attracting serious investment—more than $30 billion over the past five years—to build everything from auto and aerospace factories to five-star resorts and call centers for multinationals.

Even Algeria and Libya, long shunned on the international stage, are starting to revive their stagnant economies. Both are opening up to foreign investment and, with pipelines under the Mediterranean, have become important suppliers of natural gas to Europe as it seeks alternatives to politically unstable Russia. The Maghreb countries all "have very different politics, but they're on track, moving in the same direction," says André Azoulay, a former French bank executive who is an economic adviser to Morocco's King Mohammed VI.

The Maghreb—"place of the sunset" in Arabic—is likely to keep expanding in spite of the global economic turmoil. Growth forecasts for 2009 range from 3.7% in Tunisia to more than 5% in Libya. Euler Hermes, a consultancy that analyzes investment risk, now rates Tunisia and Morocco as safer than Hungary, Romania, and Bulgaria. "While the [Maghreb countries] will certainly be adversely affected by the downturn, they are robust enough to survive," says Euler Hermes analyst Andrew Atkinson.

The Maghreb's appeal is obvious. It's in the Continent's backyard: Tangier lies just eight miles from Spain across the Strait of Gibraltar. The region's governments are relatively stable and business-friendly. And it's cheap, with factory wages averaging $195 to $325 a month. Compare that with the average $671 monthly paid by French automaker Renault at its Dacia Logan factory in Romania.

Those numbers help explain why Renault is building an assembly plant in Tangier that will be one of its biggest anywhere. The factory is expected to employ 6,000 workers, and Moroccan officials say it could attract suppliers that would provide jobs for 35,000 more. Although the global crisis has delayed the plant's inauguration by as much as a year, Chief Executive Carlos Ghosn says Renault remains committed to the venture, which will build low-cost Logan cars for the Maghreb and beyond. "We are optimistic about these markets," he says.

Europe's aerospace industry is just as bullish on the region. Next year, Airbus plans to open a $76 million factory in Tunisia with 1,500 workers. And the industry's suppliers already employ more than 10,000 in the Maghreb, making fuselage panels, high-pressure pipes, and much more. France's Groupe Safran, for instance, has six facilities in the Maghreb employing almost 1,400 people. Inside its airy, brightly lit factory near the Casablanca airport, women in white jackets painstakingly weave electric wires into cables destined for Boeing (BA) and Airbus jets. The joint venture with Boeing and Morocco's flag carrier Royal Air Maroc employs 600 people earning an average of $315 a month. The workweek is 44 hours, considerably longer than in most of Europe. And with no unions, it's easier for managers to match production with orders by getting employees to work overtime. "We are competitive not only on salary but on flexibility and responsiveness," says Hamid El-Andaloussi, the head of Safran's Moroccan operations.

Casablanca is emblematic of the Maghreb's vigor. Far from the seedy, lawless outpost depicted in the Humphrey Bogart film that made it infamous, Casablanca is a bustling city of 4 million. Office towers overlook the walled Old Medina, an ancient district of narrow, winding streets. On the outskirts, workers are putting the finishing touches on a vast complex of office buildings called Casanearshore. It will house call centers and back-office operations for tenants such as Dell (DELL) and Paris-based bank BNP Paribas that are eager to tap the French language skills in the former French colony.

(14

النص العربي:

Arabic Text:

حروب الشطرنج:

عُرفت لعبة الشطرنج لفترة طويلة كإحدى الخطط الاستراتيجية والحرب الفكرية. ولكن في العام الماضي, انتقلت المعارك من رقعة الشطرنج إلى غرفة الاجتماعات.

حتى العام الماضي, كانت بطولة الشطرنج يحكمها الاتحاد الفيدرالي العالمي للشطرنج , ولكن بطل العالم الروسي غاري كاسباروف ومنافسه نيكل شورت من بريطانيا العظمى شعرا بالاستياء من الطريقة التي يقوم فيها الاتحاد العالمي للشطرنج باستعمال المكافأة المالية. فخرجا عن هذا الاتحاد وشكّلا اتحاد الشطرنج للمحترفين.

كان رد فعل الاتحاد العالمي للشطرنج أن جرّد كاسباروف وشورت من منزلتهما الحرفية ورفض الاعتراف ببطولة اتحاد الشطرنج للمحترفين. ومع ذلك, ومنذ تربّع كاسباروف ملكاً على بطولات الشطرنج في العام 1985, فإن معظم مشاهدي الشطرنج يتفرجون على البطولة التي تتألف من 24 مباراة على مدى شهرين ستحدد ملك الشطرنج الجديد غير الرسمي الذي لا يُنازع.

النص الإنكليزي:

English Text:

Chess Wars:

The game of chess has long been known as one of strategy and mental warfare. In the past year, however, the battles have moved from the board to the boardroom.

Until last year, championship chess was ruled by the world chess federation (FIDE). World –champion Garry Kasparov of Russia and challenger Nigel Short of Great Britain became disgruntled over the way the FIDE handled award money. They broke away from the FIDE and formed the professional Chess Association (PCA). The FIDE responded by stripping Kasparov and Short of their professional rankings and refusing to recognize the PCA championship. Still, since Kasparov has reigned as chess king since 1985, most chess watchers have their eyes on the PCA championship in London.

The 24 – game, two – month – long championship will determine the new "unofficial" chess king.

(15

النص العربي:

Arabic Text:

أعلن لاعب فريق استون فيلا الإنجليزي بول ميرسون في تصريح لهيئة الإذاعة البريطانية (بي بي سي) اعتزال اللعب دوليا.

وقال ميرسون إنه سوف يركز على اللعب مع استون فيلا مؤكدا اعتزامه الانسحاب من الساحة الدولية.

وأضاف لاعب أستون فيلا "لقد اعتزلت.. إن هذا ما كان يجب علي أن أقبله.. إنني لم أحصل على فرصة للعب الدولي".

وعبر ميرسون عن يأسه من الانضمام للمنتخب الإنجليزي الذي يستعد حاليا لأداء مباراة مع المنتخب الأرجنتيني الأسبوع المقبل.

وقال "لقد لعبت مع المنتخب ولأزال قادرا على العطاء ولكن لاعبين أصغر سنا انضموا للفريق ولذلك فهذا هو الوقت المناسب للاعتزال".

يذكر أن ميرسون شارك في تسع مباريات دولية فقط مع منتخب إنجلترا لكرة القدم ولعب احتياطيا في 12 مباراة من بينها مباراة ألمانيا عام 1991 التي سجل فيها ثلاثة أهداف. وكانت آخر مبارياته الدولية ضد جمهورية التشيك في 1998. وكان ميرسون قد ضم للمنتخب قبل مباراة فرنسا في فبراير 1999 لكنه لم يلعب وفشل منذ تلك المباراة في الانضمام للفريق مرة أخرى تحت قيادة كيفين كيغان.

النص الإنكليزي:

English Text:

Paul Merson has told BBC Sport he is quitting international football and wants to concentrate on playing for Aston Villa. Merson told BBC of his intentions to withdraw from the international scene.

Merson said: "I've retired; it's just something that I've come to accept. I never got the chance.

Merson spoke of his despair at not being in the squad for next week's game against Argentina: "I've played as well as I could and the youngsters are getting in front of me so it's time to end it." Merson only started nine games for his country, plus earned a further 12 caps for his substitute appearances including his debut against Germany in 1991, and scored three goals.

His last game in an England shirt came against the Czech Republic in 1998.

He was included in Howard Wilkinson's squad for the game against France in February 1999 but didn't play, and has since failed to feature in any of the squads named by Kevin Keegan.

(16

ترجم النص الآتي إلى الإنكليزية

Translate the following text into English

الأوراق المالية لسوق المال

الأوراق المالية لسوق المال هى أوراق دين أو أوراق ذات دخل ثابت تبلغ فترات استحقاقها عاماً أو أقل ، وعادة ما تكون استثمارات سائلة آمنة يستخدمها المستثمرون لصناديق الطوارئ, والاستثمارات قصيرة الأجل . تستخدم هذه الأوراق المالية كمناطق انتظار مؤقتة للأموال. ويمكن استثمار النقود التى لا استخدام لها فى الأوراق المالية لسوق المال من أجل الحصول على عائد. وتعد هذه الأوراق المالية استثمارات ذات خطورة أقل من الأسهم والسندات . ومع ذلك، فبالنسبة للفترات الطويلة من الزمن ، تكون عوائد الأوراق المالية لسوق المال أقل بكثير من عوائد الأسهم والسندات . وتشمل الأوراق المالية لسوق المال أذون الخزانة والأوراق التجارية وأذون الصيارفة وشهادات الإيداعات وعقود إعادة الشراء , والصناديق المشتركة لسوق المال

17) ترجم النص الآتي إلى الإنكليزية

Translate the following text into English

اجتمع وزراء المالية والعمل في مجموعة الدول الصناعية السبعة فـي ديترويـت أمـس لمناقشة قضية البطالة وهي القضية التي تعاني منها اقتصاديات هذه الدول.

وحث الرئيس الأمريكي بيل كلينتون في افتتاح المـؤتمر المشاركين فيـه علـى تحمـل مسؤولياتهم والعمل على زيادة فرص العمل في العالم.

وأصدرت القمة بيانا أكدت فيه أن تحسين التعليم هو الأساس لزيادة فرص العمل الجيدة في عصر التطورات التكنولوجية المتسارعة.

18) ترجم النص الآتي إلى العربية

Translate the following text into Arabic

Bahrain, U.S. sign treaty

Washington (Reuters): The United States has signed an investment treaty with Bahrain, Washington's first with a Gulf nation.

The so-called Bilateral investment treaty, signed by U.S. trade representative Charlene Barshefsky and Bahraini Finance Minister Abdullah Hassan Saif, would guarantee the free transfer of capital, profits and royalties, and provide other benefits to investment between the two countries.

Barshefsky said the treaty should boost bilateral trade, which already approaches $500 million a year.

"For Americans, these measures will offer additional confidence in Bahrain as a center of business and trade in the Gulf", Barshefsky said in a statement.

(19

ترجم النص الآتي إلى العربية

Translate the following text into Arabic

Japan extends its aid

MINISTER of State for Foreign Affairs and International Cooperation Fayza Abul-Naga and Japanese Ambassador to Egypt Kazuyoshi Urabi last week signed a $35 million grant agreement to finance a water project in Egypt. Japan will provide the money to pay for the second phase of Japanese- funded water supply system project in Al-Haram district. The total costs of both phases of the water project, which is expected to supply clean water to 700,000 citizens, will reach $70 million.

Abul-Naga said Egyptian-Japanese relations were progressing since the visit of Japanese Premier Junichiro Koizumi a few weeks ago. During his visit to Egypt, the Japanese premier announced that Egypt will be receiving $200 million in economic assistance from Japan to finance infrastructure and water supply projects.

The Japanese economic assistance programme to Egypt consists of three components grants, technical assistance and easy loans, Ahul-Naga said at a press conference last week.

"Since the beginning of the economic cooperation between Egypt and Japan in 1974, Egypt has received $1 billion in grants, $400 million in technical assistance and $5.3 billion in easy loans," she said.

The Japanese aid was used in financing major projects, such as the Cairo Opera House, the Suez Canal Bridge and the Abul-Reesh Children's Hospital.

The partnership agreement signed in 1999 between Egypt and Japan included the establishment of a free trade area and an Egyptian-Japanese

Business Council that aims at boosting trade relations between the two countries.

ثالثا:أخبار أدبية وثقافية وفنية

Third: Literary, Cultural and Art News

(1

النص العربي:

Arabic Text:

روبن هود:

بحسب القصة الأسطورية, كان روبن هود خارجاً على القانون يعيش في غابة شيروود, فـــي نوتينغهام شاير, وكان "يسرق من الأغنياء ويعطي الفقراء". ومن بين "الرجال المرحين" الذين تبعوه كان جون الصغير, والراهب تك, وويل سكارلت.

ربما كان هناك شخص حقيقي في القرون الوسطى يُـدعى روبـن هـود ولكـن القـصة الأسطورية تستند على الارجح إلى مغامرات قام بها عدة خارجين على القانون حقيقيين في كل من غابة شيروود وغابة بارنسديل, في يوركشاير.

اول تسجيل مكتوب لروبن يعود إلى نحو العام 1370 , فقد كان المغنّون المتجولون ينـشرون قصته الأسطورية هذه قبل ذلك بسنوات كثيرة. ولكن في نحو العـام 1450 صـارت تكتـب تمثيليات ومسرحيات عن روبن هود. ومع مجيء العام 1500 كان رجال ينتكرون بهيئة روبن في ألعاب "يوم مايو/أيار" ترافقهم فتيات يتنكرن مثل "مايد ماريون" التي أحبت حيـاة الخـروج عن القانون. وعبر القرون تغيرت غالباً أوصاف روبن, ولكن كان يُنظر إليه دائماً علـى أنـه شخص مسيحي صالح, وعدو للموظفين الرسميين المحليين والأشرار ورجال الدين الفاسـدين, ورامي سهام ومبارز بارع, وضليع بالتنكر.

النص الإنكليزي

English Text:
Robin Hood
According to legend, Robin Hood was an outlaw who lived in Sherwood Forest, Nottinghamshire. He "stole from the rich and gave to the poor". Among the "merry men" who followed him were Little John, Friar Tuck and Will Scarlet. There might have been a real medieval person called Robin Hood. But the legend was probably based on the adventures

of several real outlaws, in Sherwood Forest and Barnsdale Forest, Yorkshire.

The first written record of Robin Hood comes from the 1370s. Travelling minstrels had been spreading his legend for many years before then. By about 1450 Robin Hood plays were being put on. And by 1500 men were dressed up as Robin in May Day games, accompanied by girls dressed as "Maid Marion", the love of the outlaw's life. Over the centuries descriptions of Robin often changed. But he was always seen as a good Christian, as an enemy of wicked local officials and corrupt clergymen, as a great archer and swordsman, and as a master of disguise.

2) النص العربي:

النص العربي:

Arabic Text:

توفي والتر بايتون اعظم مهاجم في تاريخ دوري كرة القدم الامريكي ولاعب فريق شيكاغو بيرز وذلك يوم الاثنين الماضي عن عمر يناهز 45 عاما.

وكان بايتون يعاني من مرض سرطان القناة الصفراوية الذي تم اكتشاف إصابته به مطلع العام الحالي خلال علاجه من مرض نادر في الكبد.

يذكر أن بايتون أعلن في فبراير الماضي أنه يعاني من مرض في الكبد يحتاج إلى عملية زرع كبد.

وقال الدكتور غريغ جورز وهو الطبيب الذي كان يتولى علاج بايتون في مستشفى "مايو كلينيك" في مؤتمر صحفي إن بايتون أصيب فيما بعد بسرطان القناة الصفراوية وإن الورم كان متقدما جدا وينتشر بسرعة كبيرة خارج الكبد مما أدى إلى إلغاء فكرة زرع كبد جديد له.

ولم يفصح الطبيب عن تاريخ اكتشاف إصابة بايتون بالسرطان.

النص الإنكليزي:

English Text:

Walter Payton the NFL's greatest rusher, died Monday of bile duct cancer that was discovered earlier this year during his treatment for a rare liver disease. He was 45.

"HE WAS THE best football player I've ever seen. And probably one of the best people I've ever met," said Mike Ditka, who coached Payton for six years.

Payton disclosed in February that he was suffering from primary liver disease and needed a liver transplant.

His Physician, Dr Greg Gores of the Mayo Clinic, said Payton was subsequently diagnosed with cancer of the bile duct.

"The malignancy was very advanced and progressed very rapidly," Gores said at a news conference. Because the cancer had spread so rapidly outside his liver, a transplant "was no longer tenable," the doctor said.

Gores declined to say when the cancer was diagnosed.

(3

النص العربي:

Arabic Text:

استجابة قوية للتطعيم ضد شلل الأطفال

قال مسؤول صحي في إمارة الشارقة إن نحو 22 ألف طفل تتراوح أعمارهم بين شهرين وخمس سنوات تم تطعيمهم ضد مرض شلل الأطفال في الأيام الثلاثة الأولى من الحملة القومية للتطعيم.

وأوضح المسؤول إن الحملة تستهدف هذا العام تطعيم 35 ألف طفل معربا عن أمله في تحقيق هذا الهدف.

وكانت الحملة تستهدف في العام الماضي تطعيم 31 ألف طفل تم تطعيم 91% منهم.

النص الإنكليزي:

English Text:

Polio vaccinations get strong response

About 22,000 children between the ages of two months and five years have been vaccinated against polio here in the first three days of the national immunization plan. "This year we set a target of 35,000 children and we hope to achieve it," a health official said.

Last year's target was 31,000 and about 90 per cent were vaccinated.

النص العربي:

Arabic Text:

الصراعات العرقية والدينية

تسود الصراعات العرقية والاثنية دولاً أفريقيّة عدّة, ويعتبر المثال الكونغولي –
الرواندي– البوروندي مثالاً صارخاً لها, حيث تتواجه أكثرية من الهوتو مع أقلية من
التوتسي مدعومة حالياً من الولايات المتحدة.

ويعتبر هذا الصراع أكبر تحدّ لحدود الدول التي رسمتها القوى الاستعمارية في
منطقة البحيرات العظمى. فالاستعمار الغربي لم يراع التقسيمات القبلية والعرقية التي
تُعتبر واقعاً معروفاً في أفريقيا وذلك عند رسم حدود الدول.

وحتى منتصف العقد الماضي كان التوتسي بمنزلة أكراد منطقة شرق أفريقيا أي أقليّة
مهمّشة. لكنّهم وبعد أن استولوا على السلطة في بوروندي, بدأوا يحاولون إقامة
أمبراطورية التوتسي في منطقة البحيرات العظمى.

ويبقى السؤال: ماذا سيحل بالأغلبية الهوتو؟ وهل سيتّم إعادة تشكيلهم لتكوين دولة
منفصلة, الأمر الذي سيكون ربّما مخرجاً للنزاع القبلي المسلح الحالي؟

النص الإنكليزي:

English Text:

Ethnic and Religious Conflicts

Racial and ethnic conflicts dominate many African states. A glaring
example is the Congolese – Rwandan- Burundian one, where a majority of
Hutus confronts a minority of Tutsis presently supported by the United
States. This conflict is considered the biggest challenge to the state borders
drawn by colonial powers in the Great Lakes area. When drawing the
boundaries of countries, Western colonialism did not allow for tribal and
racial division, a known reality in Africa's Kurds, marginalized minority.
After seizing power in Burundi, however, they started establishing the Tutsi
Empire in the Great Lakes area.

The question remains: What will happen to the Hutu majority? Will they
be reconstituted to create a separate state, which may be a way out of the
current armed tribal conflict?

(5

النص العربي:

Arabic Text:

المخدِّرات والمراهقات

أصبحت المخدِّرات في الوقت الحاضر أسهل السبل وأيسرها لخطف المراهقات

واسترقاقهن. ويُجمع الخبراء على أن الفتيات المدمنات يبدأن بتدخين (الماريجوانا) أو

بتناول الحبوب المنعشة, وتقدَّم إليهن في أول الأمر مجاناً, على أنها جلاء للذهن وترويح

عن النفس, فإذا اعتدن عليها ازددن ولعاً بها ولا يطقن صبراً عنها, وانتقلن منها إلى

مخدِّرات أشد فتكاً, كالكوكايين والهيرويين, ويصرن أسيرات بائعيه ومروِّجيه, يُطِعْنهم

في كل أمر. فالمخدرات غالية الثمن لا يمكن لمدمنة أن تشتري القدر الكافي لحاجتها

منه, فتدفع الثمن من جسدها, وتتحول إلى رقيقة بإرادتها الظاهرة, وتُستغل في البغاء,

وقد تُنقْل من بلد إلى آخر ولا يبين لها أثر.

النص الإنكليزي:

English Text:

Drugs and Teen-age Girls

Nowadays drugs have become the simplest and easiest way to kidnap and enslave female teenagers. Experts agree that addictive girls start with smoking marijuana, or taking stimulating pills, offered to them in the beginning free of charge, as something for a lucid mind and entertainment for one's self. Once used to [drugs], they become more fond of them and can't do without them; moving [later on] to more fatal drugs such as cocaine and heroin, thus becoming prisoners of drug sellers and pushers, obeying them in every aspect. Drugs are expensive. A (female) addict cannot afford to buy a sufficient quantity to satisfy her needs; so she pays the price with her body and, by her manifested will, turns into a slave. She gets exploited in prostitution, and may be moved from one country to another with no traces left behind.

(6

النص العربي:

Arabic Text:

المستشار أبو الحسن يرحب بافتتاح مدرسة المركز الثقافي الاسلامي في نيويورك

قُبل افتتاح حضرة صاحب السمو أمير البلاد الشيخ صباح الأحمد الجابر الصباح مدرسة المركز الثقافي الإسلامي في نيويورك أمس بترحيب شديد وارتياح في أوساط الجالية العربية والإسلامية في المدينة.

وأعرب أفراد الجالية عن تفاؤلهم وأملهم بأن تقوم المدرسة بدور فعال في مجال التعليم ونشر الثقافة والقيم الإسلامية الوسطية معبرين عن شكرهم لدولة الكويت لإنشاء هذا الإنجاز الحضاري المهم.

من جانبه أعرب المستشار في الديوان الاميري محمد عبد الله أبوالحسن في تصريح لوكالة الأنباء الكويتية (كونا) وتلفزيون الكويت عن ارتياحه لتحقق هذا الإنجاز قائلا "طالما أحسست بحاجة الجالية الإسلامية لهذه المدرسة من خلال وجودي مع الجالية منذ 1981 فهي تحتاج إلى مكان للصلاة ومكان للتثقيف بالدين الإسلامي ومكان لتعليم أبنائها".

وأضاف "وقد أنعم الله علينا الآن بذلك وبحضور حضرة صاحب السمو الشيخ صباح الأحمد الجابر الصباح الذي تابع أعمال إنشاء المركز ثم إنشاء المدرسة عن كثب خلال السنوات الطويلة التي كنت أعمل فيها كمندوب دائم لبلادي في نيويورك".

وأوضح أن "الحلم تحول إلى حقيقة وأصبح لدى الجالية الاسلامية في مدينة نيويورك وأيضا لجميع المسلمين في الولايات المتحدة مركز متكامل يشتمل على مكان للصلاة ومدرسة ومركز ينشر أصول الثقافة والفقه الإسلامي والوسطية التي نحتاج إليها هذه الأيام".

وبين أن المدرسة هي آخر جزء من المشروع الذي أسسته الكويت منذ 1963 عندما تم شراء قطعة الأرض التي نحن عليها الآن بمساحة 88 ألف قدم مربع قسمت الى جزأين الجزء الأول تبلغ مساحته 44 ألف قدم مربعة بني عليه المسجد وهو مبنى ذو طابقين وقد افتتحه حضرة صاحب السمو المغفور له الشيخ جابر الأحمد الجابر الصباح تغمده الله بواسع رحمته.

وذكر أن الكويت الآن تنال فرصة أن يقوم حضرة صاحب السمو الشيخ صباح الأحمد بافتتاح الجزء الثاني من هذا المشروع الضخم وهو المدرسة التي بنيت على مساحة 44 ألف قدم مربعة.

واضاف إنه من حسن الطالع أن هذا المركز سوف يدير ويدعم نفقاته بالقيمة الإيجارية التي تتولد لدى المركز من البناية السكنية ذات ال 48 دورا التي بنيت على جزء من الأرض مقابل إيجار سنوي مبينا أن بعد 99 عاما سيعود المبنى بكامله ملكا للمركز الاسلامي.

وأوضح المستشار في الديوان الاميري أن "هدف المدرسة ليس فقط تعليم الأطفال أصول الدين الاسلامي واللغة العربية وإنما هي أيضا مدرسة نظامية سوف تبدأ من مرحلة الرياض إلى المرحلة المتوسطة وسيحصل طلبتها على شهادات تؤهلهم للدخول الى أرقى جامعات الولايات المتحدة".

وقال إن "المركز أصبح محط أنظار كل من يقصد مدينة نيويورك من القادة إذ استقبل رؤساء دول عديدين قاموا بأداء صلاة الجمعة وزاروا المركز الذي أصبح له أيضا باع طويل في بث روح الوسطية وبالذات بعد أحداث 11 سبتمبر".

وبين المستشار أبو الحسن أن المركز يستقبل منذ ذلك التاريخ الكثير ممن يريدون أن يعرفوا حقيقة الإسلام وما يتسم به من قيم التسامح والتواصل والوسطية موضحا أن المركز ينظم في مسجده أسبوعيا ندوات حضارية تجمع بين جميع الديانات ويستقبل طلبة الجامعات والمدارس.

وهنأ أبو الحسن الجالية الإسلامية ورئيس مجلس الأمناء الحالي سفير دولة الكويت لدى الامم المتحدة عبد الله المراد الذي بذل جهودا دؤوبة منذ أن تسلم رئاسة مجلس الأمناء لإيجاد الدعم والتأييد للمركز.

من جانبه قال مدير المركز زياد منير في تصريح مماثل ل(كونا) إن المدرسة تعتبر "إنجازا تاريخيا" و"حلما يتحقق" انتظرته الجالية منذ أكثر من 40 عاما.

من جهته وصف سفير الجامعة العربية لدى الأمم المتحدة يحيى المحمصاني المدرسة بأنها "عمل مجيد ومبارك نفتخر به جميعا ونقدر كل الجهود التي سمحت بإنجاز المركز والمدرسة التي ستكون عاملا ناشرا للثقافة والتعليم والمبادئ الإسلامية والروحية التي كانت تنقصنا هنا".

وأضاف "إننا نبارك الاحتفال ونأمل كل خير ونعرب عن كامل التقدير والتحية للكويت على هذا العمل الكريم".

النص الإنكليزي:

English Text:

NY's Muslim community overjoyed with inauguration
of Islamic school

The Muslim community expressed their joy Thursday evening with the inauguration of the Islamic Cultural Center of New York's Islamic School by His Highness the Amir of Kuwait, saying that it would play a major role in educating their children about Islam and its values.

Speaking to KUNA and Kuwait TV - on the sidelines of the inauguration ceremony, Kuwait's Amiri Diwan Advisor Ambassador Mohammad Abulhassan said, "I have always sensed the need of the Muslim community - whom I lived among since 1981 - for a place to pray, a place to spread awareness about Islam, and a place to teach their children".

He added, "Now, this dream has become a reality, and (took place) with the attendance of His Highness the Amir (of Kuwait) Sheikh Sabah Al-Ahmad Al-Jaber Al-Sabah, who closely followed the construction of the center, and then the school, during the years that I was here as my country's permanent representative to the UN".

Abulhassan said that the Muslim community in New York now had a comprehensive place that included a mosque, a school, and a center that spread the word on the principles of Islam "and the moderation that we need today".

The advisor explained that the school was the last part of the project that Kuwait launched back in 1963, when it purchased the piece of land measuring 88,000 square feet and split it into two segments: 44,000 square feet upon which was build a two-storey mosque inaugurated by the late Amir, Sheikh Jaber Al-Ahmad Al-Sabah; and the second 44,000 square feet upon which the school was built.

He explained that the center was financed by the rent reaped from the 48-storey residential building that was constructed on part of the land.

As for the school, he said that its aim was not only to teach children the Arabic language and principles of Islam, explaining that it would be a full-time school with classes beginning at kindergarten up to middle school, from which students would get accredited certificates.

Moreover, the center is now a place visited by heads of state and world leaders, many of whom performed the Friday prayers here, he said, adding that after the September 11, 2001 attacks, the center was known for its efforts to promote moderation and tolerance.

The center also hosts weekly seminars for people of different faiths, and also welcomes university and school students, he added.

Abulhassan congratulated the Muslim community, and thanked Chairman of the Board of Trustees Ambassador Abdullah Al-Murad of Kuwait for his efforts.

Meanwhile, the center's Director Ziyad Muneer said that the school was "a historic achievement and a dream come true," noting that the community had been waiting for more than 40 days for this day to come.

Arab League Representative to the UN, Ambassador Yahya Al-Muhmasani, meanwhile told KUNA that this was a "grand effort that we are all proud of," adding that the center and the school would play a vital role in spreading Islamic culture and teachings. He hailed Kuwait's efforts .

(7

النص العربي:

Arabic Text:

ثورة الطبقة الوسطى في الصين

بعد واحدة من أسرع الفترات نمواً في تاريخ الاقتصاد تشق الصين طريقها لتتبوأ مكانتها كواحدة من أكبر القوى في العالم .

ولقد بدأت الحكومة الشيوعية بالاعتماد على الطبقة الوسطى الجديدة من أجل تحقيق هذا، بعد أن كانت تبدي لها الاحتقار في الماضي .

ورحبت الحكومة ، منذ بداية هذا التحرك الإصلاحي في العام 1978 ، بانضمام الرأسماليين إلى الحزب الحاكم وبدأت بتطبيق ما أطلقت عليه الاشتراكية المناسبة للمجتمع الصيني .

وحددت حكومة بكين هدفاً لها أن تضاعف الناتج المحلي الإجمالي أربع مرات خلال 20 عاماً من خلال الاستفادة من التجارة الخارجية والاستثمارات والتكنولوجيا .

ومن خلال هذا المنهج ، ستكون الصين أكبر اقتصاد في العالم متفوقة على الولايات المتحدة ومستعيدة الموقع الذي شغلته لفترات طويلة في تاريخ الإنسان إن آجلاً أو عاجلاً.

ويقول الطالب ديفيد زانغ الذي عاد لتوه من هونغ كونغ إن كل شيء ممكن خلال هذه الأيام، ويضيف " كنت دائماً أحلم بالسفر إلى الولايات المتحدة والحصول على منزل جميل ذي حديقة خضراء . لكني أعتقد أن بإمكاني تحقيق ذلك في الصين بالشكل الذي يتناسب مع ثقافتي " .

النص الإنكليزي:

English Text:

The Middle Class Revolution in China

After one of the fastest periods of growth in the history of economy, China paves its way to ascend to a great stature as one of the great powers in the world.

The Socialist government has started to depend on the new middle class to achieve this, after despising it in the past.

The government, since the start of the reformations in 1978, has called the capitalists to join the ruling party, and then implemented a 'Chinese' form of Socialism that suits the Chinese people. The government in Peking has defined its target as to quadruple the total local production within 20 years via profiting from external trade, investments, and technology.

Sooner or later according to the way you see it, China will have the greatest economy in the world, far surpassing USA, and restoring the position it held for a long time in the history of Man.

The student David Zhang who has returned shortly from Hong Kong said that everything is possible these days, " I always wanted to travel to the USA, and to get a beautiful house with a green garden, but now I believe I can materialize this dream in my homeland, China, according to my cultural background", he added.

(8

النص العربي

Arabic Text:

التقدم المتفاوت للوطن العربي

غارقة بالنزاعات و مبتلاة , فإن لدى الدول العربية ال 22 الكثير من الأمور لكي ترثي لها. ومع ذلك فإنها تقوم بتقدم سريع و إن كان غير كاف في بناء مجتمعات ستنمو و تزدهر في الاقتصاد العالمي , و ستحقق الإمكانات التي يمتلكها مواطنوها. إن نجاحهم أو فشلهم سيحدد مستقبل المنطقة , كما أنه سيؤثر على الأمن الأمريكي لعقود مقبلة.

قبل 5 سنوات, نشرت الأمم المتحدة تقرير التنمية العربية فيما يتعلق ببناء مجتمع المعرفة. ذلك التقرير الذي انتشر على نحو واسع – كما أثار الجدل أيضا- وجد أن "عجز المعرفة" يهدد التطور الإنساني و النمو الاقتصادي و الإمكانات المستقبلية للمجتمعات العربية. و هذا الأسبوع قام معهد بروكنغز بنشر دراسة جديدة بالعربية تم فيها تقييم ما تغير و ما لم يتغير منذ العام 2003.

لربما كان عدم الاستقرار السياسي هو الذي يتصدر العناوين الرئيسة, و لكن التطورات في التعليم و العلوم و الصناعة و الإصلاح الاقتصادي تستحق الملاحظة. إن الوصول الى التعليم توسع بشكل واضح خلال السنوات ال5 الماضية. فالأردن تجاوز المتوسط الدولي في معدلات العلوم للمستوى الثامن لأول مرة في تاريخه. والجامعات الجديدة بما فيها فروع لجامعات عالمية معروفة في المدينة التعليمية في قطر استقطبت أعدادا متزايدة من الطلاب خلال 6 سنوات.

في العلوم و التكنولوجيا, ازدهرت المنشورات العلمية , و من بين 9 دول عربية تمت دراستها في تقرير ,003. فقد ازداد عدد براءات الاختراع فيها. و قد استثمرت مبادرات خاصة جديدة كمؤسسة محمد بن راشد آل مكتوم مليارات الدولارات في البحوث و التعليم. إن العرب يستعملون تقنيات جديدة مثل الانترنت و أجهزة الهاتف المحمول.

ما بين 2000 و 2005 ارتفعت الصادرات التقنية من الأردن و المغرب و السعودية. إن مصر توظف الآن ما يزيد على 40000 شخص في شركات تقنية معلومات محلية و أجنبية. كما أن الاقتصاد في جميع أنحاء الوطن العربي يشهد تقدما, حتى تلك الدول التي لا تملك البترول. و في تقييم مناخ العمل الدولي فإن البنك الدولي قد رتب مصر كأولى الدول التي شهدت إصلاحا كما أشار الى الإصلاحات في السعودية و تونس و الكويت و جيبوتي.

على الرغم من هذه المكاسب, فإن التقييم بعيد جدا عن هذه الصورة الوردية. إن هناك مناطق أخرى تزدهر بصورة أكبر تاركة الوطن العربي خلف ظهرها. إن النسبة المئوية من الناتج المحلي الإجمالي للبحوث و التطوير لدى ايرلندا يفوق الأردن بما يزيد على 300% تقريبا. إن هناك ما نسبته 18% من طلاب الجامعات المغربية يدرسون العلوم أو الهندسة مقارنة بنحو 40% من الطلبة الماليزيين. إن استخدام الانترنت في مصر قد ارتفع و لكن بصورة ضئيلة إذا ما قورن بالبيرو و سلوفاكيا. كما أن التجارة البينية قد ازدادت و لكنها لاتزال بمستوى النصف إذا ما قورنت بالتجارة البينية في آسيا.

و بالرغم من أن الإنفاق على التعليم مرتفع, فإن جودة التعليم لا ترتقي الى المعايير الدولية. إن الطلاب يؤدون بشكل سيىء في الامتحانات الدولية في مجالات الرياضيات و العلوم , كما أن الجامعات لا تؤهل الطلاب بشكل مناسب للعمل. كما أن نسبة التعليم بشكل عام منخفضة فهي تصل الى 83% في سوريا و 59% في اليمن و 56% في المغرب.

النص الإنكليزي:

English Text:
The Arab world's (uneven) progress
Mired in conflict, afflicted by joblessness, and flooded with images of woe, the world's 22 Arab nations have much to lament.

Yet, they are also making rapid, if insufficient, progress in building societies that will thrive in the global economy and fulfill the potential of their citizens. Their success or failure will determine the region's future. It will also influence American security for decades.

Five years ago, the United Nations published the Arab Human Development Report on Building a Knowledge Society. That widely read – and highly controversial – report found a "knowledge deficit" that threatens human development, economic growth, and the future potential of Arab societies. This week the Brookings Institution published a new study, in Arabic, that evaluates what has and has not changed since 2003.

Political instability may dominate the headlines, but advances in education, science, industry, and economic reform also deserve notice. Access to education has expanded markedly over the past five years. Jordan exceeded the international average on eighth grade science scores for the first time ever. New university campuses, including branches of world-class universities in Qatar's Education City, have enrolled more students each year for the past six years.

In science and technology, scientific publications rose. Among nine Arab countries cited in the 2003 study, patent registrations rose. Private new initiatives, like the Mohammed bin Rashid Al Maktoum Foundation, are investing billions of dollars in research and education. Arabs are embracing new technologies, such as the Internet and mobile phones.

Between 2000 and 2005, high-tech exports rose in Jordan, Morocco, and in Saudi Arabia. Egypt now employs more than 40,000 people in native and foreign information technology companies. Economies across the region have been booming, even those without oil. In an assessment of global business climates, the World Bank ranked Egypt as the world's top reformer and highlighted reforms in Saudi Arabia, Tunisia, Kuwait, and Djibouti.

Despite these gains, the assessment is far from rosy. Other regions are progressing even faster, leaving the Arab world behind. As a percentage of GDP, Ireland's research and development spending outpaces Jordan's by nearly 300 percent. About 18 percent of Moroccan university students study science or engineering, compared with 40 percent of Malaysians. Internet usage in Egypt jumped, but only slightly compared with Peru and Slovakia. And intraregional trade increased, but it is still half the level of Asia.

Though spending on education is high, the quality of education does not meet global standards. Students perform poorly on international tests in math and science. Universities inadequately prepare graduates for jobs. Literacy rates are low: 83 percent in Syria, 59 percent in Yemen, and 56 percent in Morocco.

(9

النص العربي

Arabic Text:

الإسلام والعادات والتقاليد

إذا كان الإسلام دين سلام فلماذا سوء الفهم ؟ كيف تكتسب ديانة سلام سمعة كــدين يــدعو للحرب والإرهاب ؟ تكمن الإجابة في سوء تفسير النصوص الدينية الإسلامية لكن توائم الخطط المشوهة للإرهابيين . غالباً ما يتم إساءة فهم الكلمات والعبارات التي تتكرر في وسائل الإعلام على يد الأفراد ممن يضفون عليها معاني غير صحيحة . التعتيم والإبهام المعتمد بين كلمــة " الجهاد " والأفعال الإرهابية كانت ظاهرة نتجت ممن هم غير مؤهلين في مجال الشريعة .

منذ انتهاء الخلافة العثمانية السنية عام 1924 تمزق العالم الإســلامي ، وتــسبب فقــدان الوحدة في الكثير من الصعاب التي يحاول المسلمون التخلص منها ، ومن هذه الصعاب فقــدان نشر الإسلام التقليدي الذي جعل العديد من الناس يدعون حق إعادة تفسير النصوص الإســلامية لإضفاء الشريعة على أفكارهم . أنه اتجاه للإبهام والوهم والاســتخدام الــسيىء للمــصطلحات الدينية المهمة . الإسلام التقليدي على عكس هذا يرتبط بمفهوم ما هو صحيح وواضح كــسلطة دينية متماسكة ومستمرة في نقل الحقيقة وتعتمد على الدراسة القديمة ممثلة في المذاهب الأربعة للتشريع الإسلامي . في ظل هذه التقاليد الإسلامية تبزغ البيئة الإسلامية الفعلية وتــشمل ثــراء التقاليد الخاصة بكبار علماء الدينية وإسهامهم المستنير في تقدم الحضارات .

يحث الإسلام وسنته على الإيمان والمعاملة التي تجعل من المستحيل تخيل سفك الــدماء ، فهذا حرام لمعظم مسلمي العالم مهما كانت درجة تشددهم ، لكن البعض من المتطرفين غــضوا الطرف عن هذا الركن الأساسى ألا وهو عدم إراقة الدماء في تفسيرهم الجديد للشريعة .

كما ذكر " تيم وينتر " المحاضرو أستاذ الإسلاميات في كلية اللاهوت في جامعة كيميريدج : " من الانتصارات غير المتحدث عنها وغير المحتفى بها للإسلام الحقيقي في العالم الحــديث هو حريته التامة من تدخل الإرهاب وتورطه به (...) فالجميع وحتى أعداء الإسلام يعرفــون كم هي فكرة سخيفة ربط الإسلام بالإرهاب ".

النص الإنكليزي

English Text:

Islam and Tradition

If Islam is a religion of peace - why the misunderstanding?

How can a religion of peace gain a reputation for being a religion of war and terror?

The answer lies in the way that Islamic scriptures are misinterpreted to suit perverted agendas. Words and phrases that are often repeated in the media have been misconstrued by individuals to give incorrect meanings. The deliberate blur between 'jihad' and acts of terror has been a phenomenon that has resulted from those unqualified in the science of Sacred Law.

Since the end of the Sunni Ottoman Caliphate in 1924, the Muslim world has been fragmented. The loss of unification created many difficulties from which Muslims are still trying to recover. For one thing, it has seen the loss of the promulgation of traditional Islam, which has now given way to individuals claiming the right to reinterpret Islamic texts to grant them legitimacy in their own ideas. This has seen a tendency 'toward ambiguity and the careless use of many important terms.' Traditional Islam in contrast is related to the notion of orthodoxy, clarity and authority; to continuity and consistency in the transmission of the truth. It places its reliance upon classical scholarship as exemplified in the four schools of Islamic jurisprudence. Within this tradition of Islam, a true Islamic landscape emerges, encompassing the richness of scholarly tradition and its illuminating contribution to the advancement of civilization.

Sunni Islam engenders a faith and practice that makes the taking of innocent lives unimaginable and which is shared by the vast majority of Muslims worldwide, however the radicals appear to have overlooked this pivotal pillar with their new interpretations of Sacred Law. As noted by Tim Winter, a lecturer on Islam at the faculty of Divinity at Cambridge University 'One of the unseen, unsung triumphs of true Islam in the modern world is its complete freedom from any terrorist involvement everyone, enemies included, knows that the very idea is absurd.'

(10
النص العربي

Arabic Text:

وقت التأمل

لا يمكننا لوم الدين على أخطاء من يرتكبون الجرائم البشعة باسـمه وباسـتخدام رمـوزه

يبررون جرائمهم . في كل الأديان نجد من يعلنون تمسكهم الشديد بالتقاليد ولكن يسيئون تفسير النصوص المقدسة بشدة لتتواءم مع أهدافهم .

كل التقاليد الدينية الحقيقية تدين بشدة كل أنواع العدوان والإرهاب بكل تأكيد . لا يمكننا لوم الدين بل نلوم الجنون والكراهية الذي يدفع الإرهابيين لارتكاب تلك الجرائم البشعة ، ولا يكفــي الاستنكار والتنديد هنا ، فيجب أن نسعى لاستئصال مصدر الكراهية ، ونعرف سبب الاســتياء والفوضى والغضب والمرارة والإحباط واليأس وكيف نمحو كل مـا ســبق ، و ســرعان مــا سندرك أن تلك الأمور هي من أفعال الإنسان ، لا الدين أو الله ، وهي من نتائج نظـم الحكــم التي تقمع والسياسات التي تقتل وتمحو وتدمر . تزاداد الحاجة للتقصي في مسألة الــرابط بــين الإرهاب ودعم الأنظمة الديكتاتورية وخاصة في العالم الإسلامي . الأمر لا يتعلق بــأن العــالم الإسلامي يكره الغرب أو حتى أمريكا . هناك العديد من المسلمين يعيشون في الغرب ، ومــن النفاق الاستنكار فى حوارات تتضح بالكراهية شعوباً ترحــب وتستــضيف المهــاجرين مــن المسلمين ومعظم المسلمون يدركون التشابه الكبير في الغرب مع المبــادىء الإســلامية مثــل الحرية والتسامح وحق التعليم والحريات المدنية .

يواجه مسلمو الغرب لحظة حاسمة ، و يجب على المسلمين استعادة الروح الحقيقية السمحة للإسلام بعد أن تأذى الإسلام وفقد نزاهته وكرامته على يد حفنــة مــن الإرهــابيين واهتــزت صورته أمام العالم . كما أكد " تيم وينتر " فإن التيار الإسلامي العام سيعلن على الملأ ما فــى مكنونة : " الإرهابين ليسوا بمسلمين هو استهداف المدنيين هو نفب تام للسنة الإسلامية" .

النص الإنكليزي

English Text:

Time to Reflect

We cannot blame religion for the errors of those who use its name or symbols to justify their heinous actions. All religions have had their share of people who claimed to be strict adherents of their tradition, but who actually grossly misinterpreted their sacred texts to suit their own agendas.

All true religious traditions condemn categorically any sort of act of aggression, and certainly any act of terror. Religion cannot be blamed, but the insanity and hate that drives people to commit such atrocities can be. It would not suffice to leave the condemnation there, it is up to us to seek out the root from which this hate pours forth; what are the causes of their grievances, turmoil, anger, bitterness, frustrations, and hopelessness and how can we help to eliminate them? We will soon realize that the causes are not the doing of God or religion, but merely results of regimes that oppress and policies that kill and subvert. Now more than ever there is a need to investigate the link between terrorism and the support that continues for dictatorial regimes, particularly in the Muslim World.

It is not the case that the Muslim world hates the 'West' or indeed America. There are many Muslims living in the West and it would be hypocritical to denounce in rhetoric of hate the very host country that has welcomed them. Most Muslims realize that there are many similarities extant in the West to Islamic precepts, such as freedom, tolerance, the right to education, and civil liberties.

The Muslims in the West are facing a defining moment. Muslims must recapture the true spirit of Islam, and reclaim it from those who have harmed its integrity and honor. As Tim Winter asserts mainstream Islam will be able to make the loud declaration in public that it already feels in its heart: that terrorists are not Muslims. Targeting civilians is a negation of every possible school of Sunni Islam'.

(11

النص العربي

Arabic Text:

الأنشطة الإبداعية

تعد المشاركة في الفنون من أي نوع طريقة ممتازة لتطوير وتنمية الملكة الإبداعية لديك ، ولتكوين صداقات جديدة وإتقان مهارات جديدة ، والنهوض بقوة عقلك وتقوية تقديرك لذاتك .

كما أن هناك أنشطة فنية تحوي قدرا كبيرا من التحفيز والتحدي والفائدة والمتعـــة ، فمـــن الجيد أن توجد في بيئة فنية ومن الأفضل أن تصنع الأعمال الفنية .

إذا كان هناك دورات فنية في المدرسة أو الجامعة أو النادي أو في أنشطة ما بعد الدراســة في الفن والموسيقى فأنت محظوظ لأنها متاحة لك ، لأنها لا تتوافر في مدارس كثيرة . اســتغل هذه الفرص وهي حالياً متاحة لك ، إذا كنت تحب العزف على آلة الساكسفون ولا يمكنك شراء هذه الآلة الموسيقية فأخبر معلمك لتعرف كل شيء عن البـــرامج الموســـيقية والآلات المتاحـــة للاستعارة أو الإيجار . وإذا لم يكن هذا الخيار متاحًا فاطلب تبرعـــاً مـــن الجمعيـــات الخيريـــة واتصل بالجرائد المحلية واطلب كتابة موضوعات عن سعي مدرستك لتوفير الآلات الموســـيقية والمواد الفنية والإضاءة للمسرح وجماعة التمثيل ، وجهاز ستريو محمول وســـهل التنقـــل بـــه لفرقة الرقص الإيقاعي وكل احتياجات مدرستك .

تحقق من الأمر في المؤسسات الخيرية التعليمية والفنية لترى ما هو متاح فيها ، قـــد تجـــد دورات مجانية أو منخفضة السعر في فن الخط والتصوير والرسم والرقص الإيقاعي والغنـــاء

والعزف على الكمان . هل لدى والديك أصدقاء موهوبـــون؟ ربمـــا يعطونـــك دروســـاً فـــي تخصصاتهم الفنية .

إذا عرض والداك دفع ثمن تكلفة دورة فنية فوافق على رأيهمـــا، إلا إذا كانـــت أحلامـــك مختلفة عنهما. مثال : إذان كانا يريدان منك تعلم العزف على البيانو وتريد أنت العـــزف علـــى آلة الترمبيت وموسيقا الجاز فتحدث معهما عن أحلامك واطلب منهما الدعم، وقد تقتـــرح حـــلا وسطا : إذا دفعا لك ثمن دروس الترامبيت فستتعلم البيانو العام التالي .

النص الإنكليزي

English Text:

Creative activities

Participating in the arts-any of the arts-is a great way to develop your creativity, make new friends, master new skills, boost your brainpower, and strengthen your self-esteem. In addition, it is challenging, stimulating, rewarding, and fun. It feels good to be around art, and it feels even better to make art.

If your school offers classes, clubs, and after-school programs in music or the arts, you are lucky; many schools do not. Take advantage of these opportunities while they are available to you. If you would love to play, the saxophone but you cannot afford to buy one, Tell your teacher. Schools with music programs often have instruments available to borrow or rent. If that is not an option, ask for donations from community groups. Contact local newspapers and ask them to write stories about your school's search for musical instruments…or art supplies, lighting equipment for the drama club, a portable stereo system for the dance club, or whatever else you need.

Check with community education and arts organizations to see what is available there. You may find free or low-cost courses on calligraphy, photography, drawing, top dance, singing, or playing the violin. Do your parents have talented friends? Maybe they can give you lessons in their specialties.

If your parents offer to pay for lessons, say yes…unless your dreams differ from theirs. Example: They want you to play classical piano; you want to play jazz trumpet. Talk with them about dreams. Ask for their help and support. You might propose a compromise: If they will pay for this year's trumpet lessons, you will study piano next year.

Keep in mind that it is less important to become a great performer (or painter, or writer) than it to enjoy and appreciate the activity.

(12

النص العربي

Arabic Text:

علم الكون الفيزيائي

علم الكون الفيزيائي هو فرع من فروع الفيزياء الفلكية يعنى بدراسة البنية العظمى اللامتناهية النطاق للفضاء الكوني ، ويهتم كذلك بالإجابة عن الأسئلة الأساسية التي تتعلق بالكون ووجوده وتشكله وتطوره . كما يدرس علم الكون الفيزيائي حركات الأجسام النجمية والمسبب الأول لحركة الكون. هذه الأسئلة و المجالات كانت لفترة طويلة من اختصاص الفلسفة وتحديدا علم ما وراء الطبيعة أو «الميتافيزيقيا» ، لكن منذ عهد «كوبرنيكوس» ، أصبح العلم هو من يحدد كيفية حركة النجوم و مداراتها و ليس التفكير الفلسفي. والتطور الفعلي لفهم الكون بدأ في القرن العشرين بعد ظهور النظرية النسبية لآينشتاين وتحديداً النسبية العامة التي تتحدث عن شكل الفضاء الكوني ، وخصوصا بعد التنبؤات الدقيقة التي أكدتها أجهزة الأرصاد الفلكية فيما بعد.

النص الإنكليزي

English Text:

Physical cosmology

Physical cosmology is one of the branches of cosmological physics, and it is the study of the endless structure of the outer space. Physical cosmology is concerned with finding answers to questions about the universe, its existence, formation, and development. It is concerned as well with the study of the movement of astral bodied (stars), and the First Mover of the universe. These question and fields were in the domain of philosophical studies, especially the metaphysics. However, from the era of Copernicus, it has become a science in itself, which determines the movement of the stars, their orbits, and not philosophical thought. The real development in the understanding of the universe began in the twentieth century after the appearance of the Relativity Theory by Einstein, and the general relativity that deals with the form of outer space of the universe especially after the precise predictions that were proven by the space observatory machines later on.

(13

النص العربي

Arabic Text:

هندسة الري

هندسة الري هي العلم الذي يهتم بتزويد الأراضي الزراعية بالمياه اللازمة للاســتخدامات الزراعية بطريقة محسوبة بدقة على أساس المنــاخ والطبوغرافيــا وطبيعــة التربــة (درجــة الحامضية، تدرج الحبيبات ، ...) و إمداد التربة بالماء يحافظ على نــسبة الرطوبــة اللازمــة لنمو النبات، وينقي التربة من الأملاح الزائدة ، للحفاظ على نسبة ملوحة معتدلــة فــي منطقــة جذور النبات. فمثلا يمكن زراعة الأراضي المالحه بالأرز ، الذي يحتاج لكميات ميــاه كبيــرة وبهذا الشكل يتم غسل التربة من الأملاح . يقوم الماء بإذابة المواد الغذائيــة التــي تحتويهــا التربة كي تتمكن جذور النبات من امتصاصها، ويساعد على الحفاظ على درجه حرارة التربــة المناسبة لنمو النبات ويحمل الأملاح الزائدة والمواد الضاره بالنبات إلى بــاطن الأرض وإلــى المصارف.

النص الإنكليزي

English Text:
Irrigation engineering
Irrigation engineering is a science that is concerned with providing agricultural lands with water necessary for agriculture in a meticulously calculated way depending on the climate, topography, and nature of the soil (acidity level, gradation of soil granules, ...etc.). Providing soil with water preserve the humidity level necessary for plants to grow, and washes away extra minerals from the soil to keep the suitable salinity concentration within the area of plants' roots. For example, rice can be planted in salty lands, but it needs great amounts of water, thus the excess water washes extra salts away from the land. Water is a solvent for nutrients in the soil so that roots can absorb these nutrients. Water keeps the soil temperature suitable for pants' growth, and it carries extra salts and other substances harmful to plants away to the deeper levels of soil and to ditches.

(14

النص العربي

Arabic Text:

سفن الفضاء

إذا قرأت عن سفن الفضاء التي تحمل ركابا من البشر ، فربما لاحظت أن إحدى المـشاكل التي لم يتغلب عليها العلماء بعد هي فقدان التوازن عندما يخرج الإنسان من نطـاق الجاذبيـة الأرضية .

التوازن هو القدرة على تكييف وضع الذات إزاء الكرة الأرضية التي تجـذب كـل شـيء إليها . ومن دون توازن سيكون من المستحيل على الطيور الطيـران أو الـسير للإنـسان أو وجود الحس بالاتجاهات للكائنات الحية .

لدى الإنسان عضوان للتوازن يقعان في الرأس بالقرب من الأذن . وكل عـضو كـالكيس وهو ممتلىء بالسائل الليمفاوي، وداخل كل عضو يخرج قرن استشعار يسجل كل شيء فـي خلاياه . عندما يظل الرأس قائما يتوزع الضغط على قرون الاستشعار بـشكل متـساو ، وإذا مال الرأس جانبياً يتغير الضغط على تلك القرون، والخلايا الحسية تتحفز بهذا الضغط وترسـل موجات عصبية للمخ فيغير حركة عضلات محددة ويكيف الجسم نفسه ويعود من وضع الميـل إلى وضع الانتصاب القائم.

تمكننا أعضاء التوازن من معرفة اتجاه حركتنا ، لنتخيل أننا نتحرك بسيارة للأمـام ، فـإن جسمنا يلتصق بخلق المقعد والسائل الليمفاوي في قنوات الأعضاء الخاصة بـالتوازن يميـل قرون الاستشعار للخلف ، مما يدعو الأعصاب المرتبطة به إلى إرسال رسالة تفيد بأننا نـشعر بالحركة للأمام .

بعد فترة يتحرك السائل الليمفاوي مع الجسم وقرون الاستشعار منتصبة ولا نشعر بـشعور الحركة للأمام . لنفترض أنك أوقفت السيارة فجأة ! يستمر الجسم في الاندفاع للأمـام وكـذلك السائل الليمفاوي في أعضاء التوازن وبالتالي تنحني القرون للأمام والرسالة للمخ تفيد بأننـا نبطئ.

هناك 3 قنوات داخل كل عضو من أعضاء التوازن تتوافـق مـع 3 منـاطق للقـضاء ، وبالتالي تخبرنا القرون هل نرتفع أم ننخفض ، أو هل نتحرك من جانب لآخر ، أم للـوراء أو للخلف .

النص الإنكليزي

English Text:
Spaceships
If you've been reading about space ships with human passengers, you've probably noticed that one of the problems that scientists will have to overcome is that of loss of equilibrium as a human being moves away from the pull of the earth's gravity.

Equilibrium is the ability to adjust ourselves in relation to the earth, which constantly pulls at everything that is near it. Without equilibrium, it would be impossible for a bird to fly, a man to walk, or for any living thing to have a sense of direction.

Man has two organs of equilibrium; they are located in the head near the ear. Each organ is like a sack and is filled with liquid called lymph. Inside the organ, growing out from the brain is a kind of hair that springs out of a sensory or recording cell. When the head is kept erect, the pressure on these hairs is distributed equally. If head is inclined to one side or the other, the pressure on these hairs changes. The sensory cells are stimulated by this pressure and send nerve impulses to the brain. The brain sets certain muscles into action, and the body readjusts itself and returns from an inclined to an upright position.

Our organs of equilibrium also enable us to know in which direction we are moving. Let's imagine we go out for a drive in a motor car. As the car starts forward - our body sinks back against the seat. The liquid, or lymph, in the "canals" of the organs of equilibrium, bends the sensory hairs back. This causes certain nerves with which they are connected to send a message to the brain, and we feel that we are moving forward.

After a while, the lymph moves with our body, the sensory hairs are erect, and we no longer have that feeling of suddenly moving forward. Now suppose we step on the brake! Our body keeps going forward and so does the lymph in the organs. It therefore bends the hairs forward. The message goes to the brain and we feel ourselves slowing up.

There are three "canals" in each organ of equilibrium, to correspond with the three planes of space. In this way, the sensory hairs tell us whether we're going up or down, from side to side, or backwards or forwards.

(15

النص العربي

Arabic Text:

جامعـــــــة خضــــراء

حكام أبو ظبي رأوا المستقبل، وهو مستقبل لا يتمثل في النفط. والأدلة على ذلك موجـودة فـي كل مكان في هذه الإمارة النفطية, من الألواح الشمسية البراقة، إلـى مئـات المليـارات مـن الدولارات التي استثمرت في صناديق استثمارية أجنبية متنوعة. ولكن لعل الشهادة الكبرى على مراهنة أبو ظبي على الحياة بعد النفط هو معهد مصدر للعلوم والتكنولوجيا، الذي سيتم افتتاحـه هذا الخريف. وسيكون معهد مصدر هو جامعة الأبحاث في مرحلة الدراسات العليا الأولى فـي العالم للعلوم والهندسة التي تركز على أنواع الطاقة البديلة والاستدامة ,بل وإضافة إلـى ذلـك إقامة هذه الجامعة في مدينة خضراء مكتفية ذاتيا. وفي الوقت الذي يمر فيه الاقتصاد العـالمي بفترة هبوط حاد، وفي ضوء أن أسعار النفط بلغت نصف ما كانت عليه قبل عـام فقـط، فـإن توقيـت إطـــلاق هـــذا المـــشروع لـــم يكـــن ليـصبح أفـضل. معهد مصدر اليوم ليس أكثر من الإطار الخارجي لمبنى واقع وسط غابة من رافعـات البنـاء. غير أنه حين ينتهي العمل به، سيكون حجر الأساس لمدينة المستقبل التـي تبلـغ تكاليفهـا 22 مليار دولار والتي يرتفع بنيانها من بين رمال حافة صحراء الربع الخالي في أبو ظبي. وتفاخر مدينة مصدر بأنها ستكون المدينة الودية تجاه البيئة الأولى التي يتم بناؤها من   الأسـاس لهـذا الغرض. وعلى مدى العقد المقبل، إن لم يحرف الهبوط الاقتصادي الحالي الخطط الموضوعة لها عن طريقها، ستنمو مدينة مصدر لتستضيف 40.000 ساكن, في بيئة مدينية تتغذى بالطاقة الشمسية ولا تسير فيها السيارات ولا تنتج أي فضلات وحيادية لناحية إفراز غازات الكربـون، يتصادف أنها تتربع على بعض أغنى آبار النفط على هذا الكوكب. وفكرة هذه المدينة تتمثل في قيام حكومة أبو ظبي، بالتعاون مع الشركات   التكنولوجية، بتحويل مساحة الـستة كيلـومترات مربعة التي كانت يوما أرضا قاحلة إلى مدينة على نمـط وادي الـسيليكون لناحيـة المعرفـة الخاصـــــــــــــــــــة بالطاقـــــــــــــــة النظيفـــــــة.

تأسس معهد مصدر في يونيو 2008 باستثمار على مدى خمسة أعوام تبلغ قيمتـه 1.5 مليـار دولار من حكومة أبو ظبي. والشريك الرئيسي لإمارة أبو ظبي فـي المـشروع هـو معهـد مساشوسيتس للتكنولوجيا. وحين يفتتح معهد مصدر أبوابه في 6 سبتمبر المقبل، سيكون طـاقم أساتذته والباحثون فيه قد أمضوا العام الماضي عاملين عن كثب مع أساتذة معهد مساشوسيتس للتكنولوجيا. ويتعاون معهدا مصدر ومساشوسيتس في تطوير مشاريع أبحاث مشتركة، ويقـوم

معهد مساشوسيتس بتقديم المساعدة لتصميم برامج الدراسة التي تقود إلـى حـصول الطلبـة المشاركين في هذه البرامج على الشهادات العلمية فضلا عن المساعدة على اجتذاب الصناعات التكنولوجية إلى مدينة مصدر. وفي سنته الأولى، يهدف معهد مصدر إلى توظيـف نحـو 25 أستاذا وباحثا من سائر أنحاء العالم و100 طالب، جميعهم سيدرسون بموجب بعثـات دراسـية كاملة. وسيأتي معظم الطلبة من الشرق الأوسط وشمال أفريقيا، فضلا عن بعض الطلبـة مـن الولايات المتحدة وأوروبا.

النص الإنكليزي

English Text:
A Green University
The rulers of Abu Dhabi have seen the future, and it's not oil. The evidence of that is everywhere in this petro--emirate—from gleaming solar panels to the hundreds of billions of dollars invested in diversified foreign assets. But perhaps the greatest single testament to Abu Dhabi's bet on life after oil is the Masdar Institute of Science and Technology, which opens this autumn. Masdar Institute will be the world's first postgraduate research university in science and engineering focusing on alternative energy and -sustainability—and in a self-contained green city to boot. With the global economy on edge and oil prices half what they were a year ago, the timing couldn't be better.

Today, Masdar Institute is just a shell of a building in a thicket of construction cranes. But once completed, MI will be the cornerstone of a $22 billion city of the future rising out of the sand on the edge of the Rub al Khali—or Empty Quarter—desert in Abu Dhabi. Masdar City aspires to be the world's first built-from-scratch eco--city. Over the next decade, if the economic downturn doesn't derail plans, Masdar will grow to house 40,000 -residents—in a solar-powered, car-free, zero-waste, carbon-neutral city environment that just happens to sit atop some of the richest oilfields on the planet. The idea is for the government of Abu Dhabi, in partnership with tech companies, to transform these once desolate six square kilometers into a kind of Silicon Valley of clean-energy know-how

The Masdar Institute was founded in June 2008 with a five-year investment of $1.5 billion from the Abu Dhabi government The emirate's key partner in the venture is the Massachusetts Institute of Technology. When MI opens its doors on Sept. 6, its faculty will have spent up to a year working closely with MIT professors. MIT and MI are also collaborating on the development of joint research projects, and MIT is providing assistance in designing degree programs and helping to attract tech industries to Masdar City. In its first year, Masdar Institute aims to employ about 25 faculty members from around the world and 100 students; all on full scholarships, the students will come mostly from the Middle East and North Africa, as well as Europe and the United States

(16

ترجم النص الآتي إلى الإنكليزية

Translate the following text into English:

محمد عليه الصلاة والسلام خاتم النبيين وعلاقة دعوته بالدعوات السماوية السابقة

محمد عليه الصلاة والسلام خاتم النبيين ، فلا نبي بعده ، وهذا مما أجمع عليه المـسلمون ، وعرف من الدين بالضرورة ، قال عليه الصلاة والسلام : (مثلي ومثل النبيـين مـن قبلـي كمثل رجل بنى بيتا ، فأحسنه و أجمله إلاّ موضع لبنة من زاوية من زوايـاه ، فجعـل النـاس يطوفون به ويعجبون له ويقولون هلاّ وضعت هذه اللبنة ؟ فأنا اللبنة و أنا خاتم النبيين) .

أما دعوته وعلاقتها بدعوات الأنبياء السابقين ، فقائمة على أساس التأكيد و التتمـيم كمـا يدل عليه الحديث السابق . وبيان ذلك أن دعوة كل نبي تقوم على أساسين : الأول : العقيـدة ، و الثاني :التشريع و الأخلاق . فأما العقيدة فلم يختلف مضمونها منذ بعثة آدم عليه الـسلام الى بعثة خاتم النبيين محمد عليه الصلاة والسلام ، إنما هـي الإيمـان بوحدانيـة الله تعـالى وتنزيهه عن كل ما لا يليق به من الصفات ، و الإيمان باليوم الآخر و الحـساب و الجنـة و النار ، فكان كل نبي يدعو قومه للإيمان بهذه الأمور ، وكان كل منهم مـصدقًا لـدعوة مـن سبقه ومبشرا بدعوة من سيأتي بعده ، وهكذا تلاحقت بعثتهم إلى مختلـف الأقـوام و الأمـم ليؤكد الجميع حقيقة واحدة أمروا بتبليغها وحمل الناس على الإذعان لها ، ألا وهي الدينونـة لله عز وجل وحده.

بل إنه لا يتصور أن تختلف دعوات الأنبياء الصادقين فـي شـأن العقيـدة ، لأن أمـور العقيدة من نوع الإخبار ، والإخبار عن شيء لا يمكن أن يختلف ما بـين مخبر وآخر إذا فرضنا الصدق في خبر كل منهما ، فمن غير المعقول أن يبعث أحد الأنبياء ليبلـغ النـاس أن الله ثالث ثلاثة (سبحانه عما يقولون) ثم يبعث من بعده نبي آخـر ليـبلغهم أن الله واحـد لا شريك له ويكون كل منهما صادقا فيما بلغ عن الله تعالى . هذا عن العقيدة ، أما عن التـشريع وهو سنّ الأحكام التي يتوخى منها تنظيم حياة المجتمع و الفرد ، فقد كان يختلف فـي الكيـف و الكم ما بين بعثة نبي وآخر صلوات الله وسلامه عليهم أجمعين ، وسبب ذلك أن التـشريع

من نوع الإنشاء لا الإخبار ، فلا يرد فيه ما أوردنـــاه علـــى اخـــتلاف العقيـــدة . ثـــم مـــن المفروض أن يكون للتطور الزمني و لاختلاف الأمم و الأقـــوام أثـــر فـــي تطـــور التـــشريع واختلافه ، بسبب أن أصل فكرة التشريع قائم على أساس ما تقتـــضيه مـــصالح العبـــاد فـــي دنياهم و آخرتهم ، هذا إلى أن كل بعثة نبي من الأنبياء السابقين كانت خاصة بأمة معينة ولـــم تكن عامة للناس كلهم ، فكانت الأحكام التشريعية محصورة في إطار ضيق حـــسبما تقتـــضيه حال تلك الأمة بخصوصها .

ويتضح مما سبق أنه لا توجد أديان سماوية متعددة وإنما توجد شرائع سماوية متعددة نسخ اللاحق السابق إلى أن استقرت الشريعة السماوية الأخيرة التي قـــضت حكمـــة الله أن يكـــون مبلغها هو خاتم النبيين و الرسل أجمعين . أما الدين الحق فواحد ، بعث الأنبياء كلهم للـــدعوة إليه و أمر الناس بالدينونة له منذ آدم عليه السلام إلى محمد عليه الصلاة والـــسلام، ألا وهـــو الإسلام .

(17

ترجم النص الآتي إلى العربية

Translate the following text into Arabic:

Antibiotics

Antibiotics are chemicals. When these chemicals are put into the body, they kill or stop the growth of certain kinds of germs. They help your body fight disease.

The name "antibiotics" was first applied to these medicines in 1942. It comes from two Greek words meaning "against life". Antibiotics work against the forms of life that we call germs.

Many antibiotics are made from microbes. Microbes are tiny living things. For example, bacteria and molds are microbes. The microbes used in making antibiotics are chosen for their ability to produce chemical that wage war on the microbes of disease. In other words, man takes advantage of the struggle that goes on in nature among microbes.

Microbes are engaged in a constant struggle for survival. In the course of this struggle, microbes produce complex chemicals in their bodies. By investigating the chemical products of microbes, scientists have discovered many chemicals that kill disease germs. If these chemicals can be made in laboratories; and made in large enough quantities; they may be used to make antibiotics.

How do antibiotics cure diseases? How do they get to the right part of the body to go to work there? Strangely enough, science still doesn't know the answer. How does an antibiotic stop the growth of certain germs? Some scientists believe that antibiotics cut off the germs' supply of oxygen. Without oxygen, germs cannot go on dividing. Others think that an antibiotic prevents germs from taking in food from the patient's body, so the germ starves to death. Still others believe that the germ mistakes the antibiotic for part of its usual diet. The germ "eats" the antibiotic and is poisoned.

Probably antibiotics work in various ways. One antibiotic may act different ways against different germs. It may kill the germs in one case. In another, it may only weaken the germs and let the body's natural defenses take over.

CHAPTER TWO

TRANSLATION FOR CINEMA AND TELEVISION

2.1: Translating Movies and Other TV Programs

النص الإنكليزي

English Text:

LIZZIE
Ooh!
Nice one, Gordo.

GORDO
This is Gordo's house.

LIZZIE
Who talks like that?

ETHAN
Give me the rock

MIRANDA
Etan does.

TOON LIZZIE
I'm not a big fan of gym--
especially basketball --
but when the opportunity
to guard Ethan Craft comes up,
you take it.

MIRANDA
Miranda's got game.

LIZZIE
I want game.

GORDO
Our game is busy guarding Ethan.

TOON LIZZIE
True, but it's worth
every second.

GORDO
All right, watch and see
how it's done.

LIZZIE
Uh…
is that how it's done, Gordo?

GORDO
How did he do that?

ETHAN
Maybe next time,
little man.

LIZZIE
Is there anything Ethan
can't do?

GORDO
Yeah, count past ten
without taking his shoes off.

TOON LIZZIE
But if he was cute and smart
he'd be super Ethan
and I don't think the universe
is ready for that.
But I am.

GORDO
Can we talk
about something else?

LIZZIE
How about who Ethan's going
to ask to the dance Friday.

MIRANDA
You.

TOON LIZZIE
Me! Me! Me! Me! Me! Me! Me!
I mean, I-I don't care.
Whatever

GORDO
Oh, I doubt he's going
to ask you guys.

LIZZIE
Gordo!

MIRANDA
Gordo!

TOON LISSIE
It's probably true,
but he doesn't have to say it.

MIRANDA
You're just saying that
' cause you don't have
a date for the dance.

GORDO
Look, middle school's hard enough
without the added pressure
of who I'm taking
to the dance.

LIZZIE
So, I guess
we're all three
going together?
Cool.

MIRANDA
I guess it's just
the three amigos flying solo.

Arabic Text:

النص العربي

ــ رمية جيدة يا (غوردو)
ــ هذا بيت (غوردو)

ــ من يتكلم هكذا ؟
ــ أعطني الكرة

(إيثان)

لست من محبي الرياضة
وبخاصة كرة السلة

ولكن عندما تأتي فرصة حراسة
(إيثان كرافت) يجب انتهازها

ــ اللعب مع (ميراندا)
ــ أريد اللعب

مهمتنا حراسة (إيثان)

صحيح , ولكن الأمر يستحق

انظروا كيف أفعل ذلك

ــ هكذا نلعب يا (غوردو) ؟
ــ كيف فعل ذلك؟

ربما في المرة المقبلة أيها الصغير

أهناك ما لا يستطيع (إيثان) عمله؟

نعم , العد لما بعد العشرة من دون
أن ينزع حذاءه

إذا كان وسيما وذكيا فهو
إذن (سوبر إيثان)

ولا أعتقد أن العالم جاهز لذلك
ولكن أنا جاهزة

أيمكننا التحدث عن موضوع آخر ؟

من التي سيدعوها (إيثان) للرقص
يوم الجمعة ؟

أنت

أنا , أنا , أنا

أعني .. لست أبالي

لا أعتقد أنه سيدعو أيا منكما

ربما كان ذلك صحيحا , ولكن لم يكن
هناك داع لأن يقوله

إنك تقول ذلك لأنك لا تجد
من يرافقك للرقص

المدرسة صعبة وليست في حاجة
إلى ضغوط إضافية

ــ عن من سأصطحبها للرقص ؟
ــ سنذهب نحن الثلاثة معا إذن ؟

أعتقد أننا سنكون الأصدقاء الثلاثة بمفردنا

A city between the Orient and the Accident
Official population: 12 million.
A city suffocates in the traffic.
It has the oldest subway in the world.
On every one of its seven hills a Mosque stands.
Scarves and mini skirts.
An international and believer city:
Istanbul is a very old city. It was so powerful in the 6th century that she
controlled from here, the shipping in the Black Sea.
In Roman times she was the Capital of the empire.
The water supply of the Antique Metropolis was guaranteed through
Aqueduct. One of these, are still in good condition.
Under the reign of the emperor Constantine, the city was called
Constantinople. The hippodrome was its centre. This magnificent square is
today, the centre of the historic quarter Sultan Ahme't.
Three antique columns decorate this former race track, they witness to the
power and the expansion of the east Roman Empire.
This stadium use to receive 100.000 persons.

جولة في الفن

اسطنبول

مدينة بين الشرق والغرب

عدد سكانها الرسمي (12) مليون

مدينة تختنق بالازدحامات المرورية

وفيها أقدم قطار أنفاق في العالم

وعلى كل تل من تلالها السبعة يقوم مسجد

الحجاب والتنورة القصيرة

مدينة عالمية ومدينة إيمان

اسطنبول مدينة قديمة جدا وكانت قوية جدا في القرن السادس

لدرجة أنها كانت تسيطر على حركة الشحن في البحر الأسود

في العصر الروماني كانت عاصمة الإمبراطورية

كان إمداد المدينة القديمة بالماء مضمونا عبر قنوات

ما زالت إحداها في حالة جيدة

تحت حكم الإمبراطور (قسطنطين)

كانت المدينة تسمى (القسطنطينية)

ومضمار السباق كان مركزها

هذا الميدان الرائع هو اليوم مركز الجزء التاريخي للسلطان (أحمد)

(3) أعمدة أثرية تزين مضمار السباق السابق

شاهدة على قوة واتساع الامبراطورية الرومانية الشرقية

هذا الاستاد كان يتسع لمئة ألف شخص

ثانيا – أمثلة وتعابير

2.2: Sayings and Expressions

وهذه أمثلة من ترجمة التعابير الدينية وبعض الأمثال الشعبية الدارجة في عدد من الدول
العربية:

The following is a list of some of the religious expressions and some of
the public sayings which are common in some of the Arab countries:

- No power saves with God.

لا حول ولاقوة إلا بالله

- To God we belong and to him is our return.

إنا لله وإنا إليه راجعون

- I seek refuge to God from the evil spirit, the accursed.

أعوذ بالله من الشيطان الرجيم

- In the name of God, Most Gracious, Most Merciful.

بسم الله الرحمن الرحيم

- Peace be upon you!

السلام عليكم

- Likewise.

وعليكم السلام

- May God exalt your reward!

عظم الله أجرك (من اللهجة الكويتية)

- May God honor your consolation!

أحسن الله عزاءك

أقوال مقاربة:

Semi-equivalent sayings:

- The leopard cannot change its spots.

بوطبيع ما يغير طبعه ـ مثل كويتي

- Silence gives consent.

السكوت علامة الرضا

- Necessity is the mother of invention.

الحاجة أم الاختراع

- Ready for all eventualities.

مستعد لكل الاحتمالات

- First come, first served.

من سبق لبق ــ مثل كويتي

- Spare the rod, spoil the child.

نعم المؤدب العصا

- Strike while the iron is hot.

دق الحديد وهو حامي ــ مثل كويتي

- Call a spade a spade.

يقول للأعور أعور بعينه

- Man proposes, but God disposes.

العبد بالتفكير والله بالتدبير

- Beggars cannot be choosers.

طرار ويتشرط ــ مثل كويتي

- The lowest ebb is the turn of the tide.

ما بعد الضيق إلا الفرج

- Blood is thicker than water.

الدم ما يصير ماء

- Diamonds cut diamonds.

ما يفل الحديد إلا الحديد

REFERENCES

(1) Lisan Al-Arab (Tongue of Arabs), Ibn Manzhoor, 1st Edition/ 1996/ Dar Ihiaa Al-Torath, Beirut: 2/26.

(2) Translation and Its Problesm, Ibrahim Khorshid, P.P. 7-11.

(3) Al-Mofeed in Translation and Transliteration, Ghassan Ghossen, Dar Al-Ilm Lil-Malayeen, P.P. 20-24.

(4) Trend of Translation in Renaissance, Latif Zaitooni, P.P. 39-41.

(5) Translation into Arabic, Dr Mohammad Didawi, : 55.

(6) To be revised: Al-Mofassal in History of Pre-Islamic Arabs, Dr Jawad Ali: 6/669-680.

(7) Al-Mofassal in History of Pre-Islamic Arabs: 2/11 – 12.

(8) Jamharat of Arabs' Poetry, Mohammad Abu Al-Khattab Al-Qurashi: 180.

(9) Umaiya bin Abi Al-Sallt: Biograhy and Poetry: 160-161.

(10) Hamasat (Enthusiasm) of Abi Tammam, Habib Al-Ta'ee: 1/29.

(11) Explanation of Imraa Al-Qais Anthology: 125.

(12) Al-Mofassal in History of Pre-Islamic Arabs, Dr Jawad Ali: 2/694 – 732.

(13) Al-Mofassal in History of Pre-Islamic Arabs: 2/11-12.

(14) Al-Khab'a: Every thing that is hidden and concealed, Lisan Al-Arab, Ibn Manzhoor: 2/1085.

(15) Zad Al-Ma'aad fi Hoda Khair Al-Ibad, Ibn Al-Qaiyem, 3/691.

(16) Asad Al-Ghaba fi Maa'refat Al-Sahaba, Ibn Al-Athir, 2/126-127.

(17) Research: Contribution of Riqqa and Diaar Madhar in Translation, Mohammad Mohammad, Annual 16th Conference Researches for History of Sciences with Arabs, 1982: 109 – 110.

(18) For further reading: To be revised: Islam and Orientalists, P.P. 6-13, Al-Farooq: 400 – 428, Muslims and Modern Science: 31-45, Educational Methodology in Prophetic Era: 32-47, History of Arabic Literature, Carl Proclman: 4/111.

(19) Al-Fehreset (Index), Ibn Al-Nadeem, P.P. 680 – 681.

(20) Plans of Levant, Mohammad Kurd Ali, 6 / 24-25.

(21) Libraries in Islam, Mohammad Maher Hamada, P.P. 42-43.

(22) Fehrest (Index), Ibn Al-Nadeem: 131.

(23) Beginnings of Translation in Umawi Era, Lutf Allah Al-Qaderi, 162.

(24) History of Arab Thought Development in Translation from the Greek, Ismail Mazhar, Al-Muqtatef Magazine, Issue 1/ 1925: 9 - 10.

(25) Collections of Essays by Scholar and Scientist Shibli Al-No'man Al-Hindi: 6/ 7 – 8.

(26) Fehreset (Index): P.P. 301 - 307.

(27) Fehreset: 124.

(28) Tabaqat Al-Umam (Strata of Nations): P.P. 47 – 48.

(29) Fehreset (Index): 352.

(30) Story of Civilization, Durant, 13/177.

(31) Uyoon Al-Anbaa fi Tabaqat Al-Atebbaa, Ibn Abi Usaibi'aa, 260.

(32) Same Reference: 493.

(33) Ilm Al-Kalam (Scholastic Theology): 1/49.

(34) For further reading to be revised: Sciences and Arts with Arabs and their Role in World Civilization, Sayed Radhwan Ali, P.P. and Islamic Civilization in Baghdad in the Second Half of Fifth Hijri Century, Mohammad Hussain Shanab, P.P. 239 – 240.

(35) Translation Trend, Zaitooni, P.P. 14-17.

(36) History of Translation and Cultural Tend in Egypt in Reign of Mohammad Ali, Jamal Al-Din Al-Shaiyal, P.P. 211- 212.

(37) Translation in the Old and Modern Age, Shehada Al-Khoori, P.P. 77 – 85.

(38) Trend of Translation in Abbassi Era, Orank Al-A'azhami, P.P. 46-51.

(39) Tranlsation in the Old and Modern Days, Shehada Al-Khoori, different parts.

(40) Art of Translation, Mohammad Awadh Mohammad, 1961, P. 29.

(41) Translation in the Old and Modern Times, Previous Reference, P.P. 47 – 49.

(42) Translation Trend, Previous Reference, P.P. 7—75.

(43) http://www.annabaa.org/nbanews/69/025.htm

(44) Translation and Its Problems, Previous Reference, P.P. 55-65.

(45) For further reading: Translation, Dr Ali Al-Namla, Previous Reference, P. 200 – 203.

(46) Jalal Al-Din Mazhar, Islam Civilization and Impact on World Growth, P. 268 – 299 .

(47) Roget Garodi, Beyond Islam, Translated by Qusai Atasi and Michelle Wakim, 1983, P. 137.

(48) Al-Ebar : 5/543.

(49) Library in Medieval Ages, Thompson, P. 260 – 261.

(50) Translation in Old and Modern Ages, Shehada Al-Khori, Previous Reference, P. 64 – 67.

(51) Al-Mofeed in Trnaslation and Transliteration, Antoine Abdullah, Dar Al-Anwar, Damascus, Ed. 2, 2003, different places.

(52) Media Translation, Mohammad Hosni Nasser, Al-Fallah Library, Ed. 1, 2001, P. 16 – 59.

(53) Environmental Media, Abdulllah Badran, P. 51 -63.

(54) http:///www.annabaa.org/nbanews/69/025.htm (1)

(55) Al-Mofeed in Trnaslation and Transliteration, Antoine Abdullah, Dar Al-Anwar, Damascus, Ed. 2, 2003, different places.

(56) Media Translation, Mohammad Hosni Nasser, Al-Fallah Library, Ed. 1, 2001, P. 16 – 59.

(57) Environmental Media, Abdulllah Badran,P. 51 -63.

(58) http:///www.annabaa.org/nbanews/69/025.htm (1)